THE COMING OF GODOT

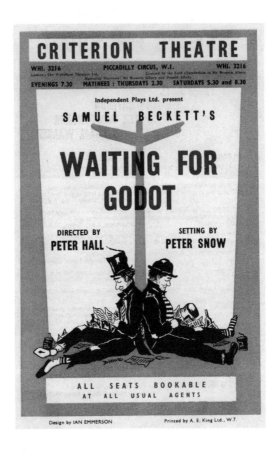

Above: the poster for Peter Hall's original production of *Waiting for Godot*, after its move from the Arts to the Criterion Theatre.

Jonathan Croall

THE COMING OF
GODOT

A Short History of a Masterpiece

OBERON BOOKS
LONDON

First published in 2005 by Oberon Books Ltd
521 Caledonian Road, London N7 9RH
Tel: 020 7607 3637 / Fax: 020 7607 3629
e-mail: info@oberonbooks.com
www.oberonbooks.com

A catalogue record for this book is available from the British
Library.

ISBN: 1 84002 595 6

Cover photographs © Nobby Clark (front)
                  © V&A Images / Theatre Museum (back)

Printed in Great Britain by Antony Rowe Ltd, Chippenham

Contents

Acknowledgements

I must first thank most warmly Peter Hall, who allowed me complete and unfettered access to the rehearsals of his fourth production of *Waiting for Godot*, and generously found time to talk about it as it evolved, both in London and in Bath. I also owe a great debt to the actors, Alan Dobie, Richard Dormer, James Laurenson and Terence Rigby, for letting me observe them in rehearsal, and for patiently answering my questions about their work. I would also like to thank other members of the creative team, Kevin Rigdon, Cordelia Monsey, Peter Mumford, Trish Rigdon and Gregory Clarke, for their valuable assistance, and Nicky Palmer and Emma McDermott at the Theatre Royal, Bath.

Many other people helped me with the book, either by agreeing to be interviewed, sending me information, or putting me in touch with sources I might not otherwise have found. My thanks go to Walter Asmus, Timothy Bateson, Lesley Bruce, Robert Butler, Des Cave, Gavin Clarke, David Collison, Nora Connolly, David Drummond, Julian Glover, Lyn Haill, Tamara Hinchco, Ronald Harwood, Alec McCowen, Brian McFarlane, Barry McGovern, Braham Murray, Tony O Daleigh, Anthony Page, Lynne Parker, Trevor Peacock, Struan Rodger, Michael Rudman, Peter Sheridan, David Storey, Tom Stoppard, Colin Welland and Caroline Williams.

Finally I would like to thank James Hogan at Oberon Books for commissioning the book, and Ian Higham and Stephen Watson for their careful and efficient work during its production.

Preface

As this book goes to press the number of books by or about Samuel Beckett has risen to 335. A whole publishing industry has grown up around his name, perhaps only rivalled by the one which surrounds Shakespeare. There are academic analyses of every conceivable aspect of his work; there is even a *Journal of Beckett Studies*. So what is the justification for adding yet another book to the pile?

I believe this one is distinctive in the way it mixes on-the-spot reportage with history. In observing Peter Hall's latest production of Beckett's masterpiece, I have tried to document faithfully and in detail the way a great director and a talented group of actors met the many challenges that *Waiting for Godot* offers. At the same time, I have found it both fascinating and instructive to discover what other companies have done with this extraordinary play, and how it has influenced other playwrights. I have tried therefore to give a little of the flavour of the many and varied productions that have been staged, not just in the UK but in many different cultures and settings.

I have organised the book so that the two main elements are interwoven. I believe the best way to read it is in the order the chapters are arranged, so that the past and the present feed into each other. But it is also possible, by reading alternate chapters, to follow only the story of Peter Hall's production, or to concentrate solely on the play's stage history.

Foreword by Peter Hall

This book by Jonathan Croall is a rarity. The process of rehearsal is at its best mysterious and exciting; at its worst, it is just plain boring. Lines of communication are quickly established between the director and each of the actors. Those communications are subtly different according to the personality and needs of each individual. They are often private and incomprehensible to the spectator. To drop in on rehearsal now and then can be a confusing and misleading experience. To record the process accurately and understand the growth of the work, the observer should be there all the time.

Jonathan Croall has been at virtually all the rehearsals of my fiftieth anniversary production of *Waiting For Godot*. He has watched its growth and its tiny convulsions. He has seen how last week's weakness has developed into this week's strength. And he has seen how general notes such as 'pick up your cues quickly' can lead to a gain in energy but a loss of comprehension.

Jonathan has been an enthusiast for our work and I don't believe you will get much closer to the rehearsal process than this. So on behalf of the cast (Alan Dobie, Richard Dormer, James Laurenson, Terence Rigby), Cordelia Monsey (my associate director), and myself, I thank him for his care and understanding.

Let me put this great play in context and try to remember how it struck me when it landed on my desk fifty years ago. In 1955 I was 24 years old and a very lucky young man. I had been given a theatre (the Arts Theatre in Great Newport Street in London) and charged to provide it with a play every four weeks. The resources were minimal and the money was not good (£7 a week and luncheon vouchers); but the opportunity to direct new plays seemed too good to be true.

Then *Godot* came – literally. In the early summer, I found a script waiting on my desk. Donald Albery, a leading West End impresario, informed me that he could persuade no actor to be in *Godot* and no director to direct it. It was still running in a small theatre in Paris. Beckett had now translated it and Albery wondered if I would like to do the English-language world premiere. I ransacked my memory. The name was faintly familiar. There were novels, I knew, and I seemed to remember a connection with James Joyce.

I read the play and responded warmly. I decided to do it. I won't claim that I immediately saw it as a turning point in twentieth-century drama: that realisation came later. And it certainly took a month of intensive rehearsal for me to understand that the play was an out-and-out masterpiece. From the very beginning I thought it was blindingly original, turning the undramatic (waiting and doubt, perpetual uncertainty) into tense action. It was exquisitely constructed with an almost musical command of form and thematic material. And it was very funny. It took the cross-talk tradition of the music hall (celebrated by Laurel and Hardy and still rich in memory thanks to Morecambe and Wise) and made it into poetry. We are ridiculous, even comical when we quarrel with our partners: yet we can be compassionate and tender when we care for them. Assuredly we pass the time better in company, amusing each other with 'little canters'. They may be love scenes or fights.

The initial reception of the play was not good (Bernard Levin called it 'a really remarkable piece of twaddle') but Harold Hobson, the critic of *The Sunday Times*, found himself on the theatrical road to Damascus. He then wrote about the play for the next half-dozen Sundays.

Godot-mania gripped London. It was discussed, praised, analysed and abused. Cartoons were drawn about it, *Panorama* discussed it; Malcolm Muggeridge derided it. And it was analysed as an allegory of the Cold War.

But metaphor had repossessed the theatre and the way had been made straight for Harold Pinter, Tom Stoppard, Joe Orton and subsequent generations.

10

It is often thought that 1956 and the first night of John Osborne's *Look Back in Anger* was the reinvention of British theatre. It is certainly true that Osborne changed the times: young writers saw that they could use the theatre to write about life as they lived it. So out went the slim volumes of verse and the imitations of Kingsley Amis' *Lucky Jim*. The vigorous Royal Court revolution was well and truly under way. All this was wonderful, but it was nonetheless faintly parochial, which *Godot* certainly was not. *Look Back in Anger* was a play formed out of the naturalistic theatre of the thirties and the cosy craft beloved of the old repertories. It now seems dated.

By contrast *Waiting For Godot* hasn't dated at all. It remains a poetic masterpiece transcending all barriers and all nationalities. It is the start of modern drama. It gave the theatre back its potency and its poetry. It began a process of returning theatre to its metaphorical roots. And this process continues to this day. *Godot* challenged and defeated a hundred years of literal naturalism where a room was only considered a room if it was presented in full realistic detail, with the fourth wall removed. Godot provided an empty stage – with a tree and two figures who waited and survived. You imagined the rest because in this world of pure theatre less was definitely more. The stage was an image of life passing – in hope, in despair, in companionship and in loneliness.

I have directed *Godot* four times. Every time I do it, it becomes less obscure. On this attempt, it was as clear as clear water. How stupid it seems now that fifty years ago people denied that this play was a play. But I suppose that new tunes are always by definition unfamiliar and disturbing. From that August evening in London in 1955 the play went everywhere. It is no exaggeration to say that it went round the world, and its success continues.

In this version of *Godot*, which was performed at the Theatre Royal Bath in August 2005, it seemed to me that we were closer to realising the whole play than we had ever been. But sadly this production was only played eleven

Prologue

A basement. An empty space. Morning.

It's London in the summer of 2005. In a community centre in Clapham rehearsals are about to begin for a production of Samuel Beckett's acknowledged masterpiece *Waiting for Godot*. Two of the actors have appeared in the play once before; the other two are new to it. For the director it's a special moment, and a journey back in time: fifty years ago almost to the day he was starting to rehearse the first English production, quite unaware of the extraordinary impact the play was to have on the theatrical landscape, not just in Britain but all over the world...

Re-wind to London in the summer of 1955. Peter Hall, not long out of university and only twenty-four, is running the Arts, a small experimental London theatre just off the Charing Cross Road. One day he receives a dog-eared script of a play from a leading theatre manager, asking if he'd like to put it on at his theatre. The play is about two men, Vladimir and Estragon, waiting by a tree in an empty landscape to keep an appointment with a Mr Godot, who never appears. While waiting they argue, joke, philosophise, indulge in cross-talk, try out comic routines, insult each other, and eat a carrot or two. Once in each of the two acts they are interrupted by two other men, Pozzo and Lucky, apparently a master and his slave, and by a young boy, who tells them Mr Godot will come tomorrow, but not today. Although he doesn't fully understand it, Hall finds the play original, funny and beautifully written, and decides he will direct it himself. He is only dimly aware of Beckett's existence, and has not seen the original production of the play, written in French by an Irishman living in Paris...

Re-wind to Paris in the winter of 1952–3. Samuel Beckett's *En attendant Godot* finally makes it to the stage, opening at the tiny Théâtre de Babylone on the Left Bank. It has been a struggle to get it accepted for production, and Beckett has often despaired of finding a sympathetic manager. Several have turned down the play on the grounds that it is either incomprehensible, boring, too highbrow or too deep. But one man who has seen its potential is the director Roger Blin. It is like no other play he has come across, and he feels he has to direct it...

Re-wind to Paris in the winter of 1948–9. Early in October, in his flat on Rue des Favorites, Beckett puts aside his novel *Malone meurt* (*Malone Dies*) and as a relaxation starts to write a play. With little practical knowledge of the theatre, he finds writing for the stage 'a marvellous, liberating experience', likening it to plotting a game of chess. At first he is unsure what names to give to certain characters: Estragon is first called Levy, and Pozzo and Lucky simply *le grand* et *le petit*. He writes quickly in longhand in an exercise book, inserting into the dialogue snippets of conversation from his own life, bits of songs, references to books he has read, exchanges in the style of the music-hall, and expressions that he uses in his everyday speech. He doesn't visualise how the play might work on the stage, but simply writes lines that he thinks look good on paper.

On 29 January 1949 the play is finished, and Beckett makes a typed copy. His partner Suzanne Descheveaux-Dumesnil begins hawking it round potential producers. Within a few weeks it has been rejected by six theatrical managements. It is, Beckett says, as hopeless as giving it to the concierge...

1 The Readthrough

Monday 4 July

In the main rehearsal room in the Clapham community centre, I am sitting at a table with Peter Hall, the *Waiting for Godot* cast, the creative team, members of the stage management, and Danny Moar, the director of the Theatre Royal in Bath. The production is to open in Bath in just over seven weeks' time, as part of the Peter Hall Company's third season in the city. It is the fourth time he has directed the play, the most recent productions being at the Old Vic in 1997 and the Piccadilly in 1998.

Before the actors – James Laurenson, Alan Dobie, Terence Rigby and Richard Dormer – start on the readthrough of the play, Peter offers some preliminary thoughts.

It is of course impossible for me to completely start again on this play, and to say there won't be similarities to my two most recent productions. At the same time I don't like the word revival: it sounds as if you're breathing air into a corpse. So I want to go back to what we did before, and then change it. The main problem will be to bring the verbal and physical life together, so we must do that as soon as possible.

It's a play I feel I'd like to re-visit every five or ten years, it's that good. It's very poetic, very ambiguous, and it changes its meaning from decade to decade – as it should, because every work of art has that quality of being many-faceted. It comes out differently every time I do it, because it's different times, different actors, different audiences, different stages – and I'm different, though I don't know how.

Great theatre is always a metaphor. All we know here is that there are two men on a road by a tree, waiting for someone to turn up. It's a great metaphor for living, for the search for faith, for purpose. But I think it's erroneous to think there's a single meaning – a metaphor is a metaphor, and it means different things to different people. If you said to Sam, What does this mean?, he would reply, What does it say? By that he meant, What does it mean to you?, not what it might mean to him. He wouldn't get into that area at all.

People are disturbed by the play, because it has a very realistic pessimism about it. Yet it's so pessimistic that it ends up being optimistic: people come out feeling better because they have gazed at human reality. The reason I think is the courage of the two men, waiting day by day, and the humour, which is very heart-warming.

The script we're using is the one printed in *The Beckett Notebooks*. Sam went on chipping away at the text, cutting some of the more absurdist material, and this represents his final thoughts. He made a lot of alterations, and it's the play in its most sinuous form: it's more coherent than earlier versions, it avoids the ridiculous. It's lovely how he's stripped it down, and taken all the weeds out.

The main components of the play are the extraordinary metaphysical language of the writing, and the body language of the action. Beckett loved mime, he loved clowns, and a lot of the play is about mime. Another component is the humour, and what I've got to do in the coming weeks with you is to make the comedy and all the cross-talk precise, as precise as if I were working with Morecambe and Wise.

As a director I think it's terribly important that we don't make what Pinter describes as 'a bit of statement'. A statement is not usually ambiguous, it usually enforces its meaning. *Godot* doesn't do that: like all great plays it's essentially ambiguous, so you've got to allow many possibilities to come in for it to be credible. I say credible rather than truthful, because I like less and less the word truthful. There's nothing true about the theatre, it's artificial, that's the point of it. Whereas credible it can be.

He then suggests that the actors read the play, and that all except Terence Rigby, who's playing Pozzo, use Irish accents. Rigby and Alan Dobie as Estragon are repeating the roles they played in the 1998 production, and their assurance is soon obvious. But as Act 1 is worked through, the other two actors quickly enter into the spirit of the piece. James Laurenson as Vladimir shows great energy, and in the exchanges with Estragon there are all the signs of a good rapport, the two actors making continual eye contact in order to pick up the cues speedily. Richard Dormer rattles through Lucky's extraordinary monologue with astonishing pace and accuracy, while Terence Rigby's measured reading of Pozzo already exhibits considerable menace.

'I love the energy and speed, but it's a little too fast for comfort,' Peter says between the acts. 'A lot of it is in the pauses, but you have to earn those pauses.' The actors start to take this criticism on board during the reading of Act 2. Once they finish, costume designer Trish Rigdon passes round some preliminary costume sketches, and designer Kevin Rigdon unveils the set model. It's an appropriately simple set: a road, a tree and a rock, with a moving panel in the dark-blue background that will open at the end of each act to reveal the moon.

Finally, Peter raises the question of the rehearsal schedule. This week is going to be tricky for the actors. The first two plays in the Bath season, *Private Lives* and *Much Ado About Nothing*, are now previewing, and will have their press showings on Wednesday, which Peter will have to attend. The second two, Shaw's *You Never Can Tell* and *Waiting for Godot*, he plans to rehearse in tandem, 'an idiotic position to put myself in', he confesses. As the Shaw play will start previewing a week earlier than the Beckett, he will focus on *You Never Can Tell* this week, leaving his assistant director Cordelia Monsey to do some basic groundwork with the *Waiting for Godot* company. A matter then of Waiting for Peter...

2 Down-and-Outs in Paris

'Becket does not want his actors to act' – Jean Martin,
the original Lucky

In 1949 Roger Blin, a stage and screen actor well steeped
in the avant-garde, was just beginning his career as a director in Paris. A friend of the theorist Antonin Artaud, Blin
had been alerted to the existence of *En attendant Godot*
by the Dada artist Tristan Tzara, who had read and admired
the play, and advised Beckett to show it to Blin. Beckett's
partner Suzanne Descheveaux-Dumesnil duly took the script
round to the Théâtre Gaîté-Montparnasse where Blin was
working. Blin thought it highly original, a play that seemed
to question the very basis of theatre. He loved its mixture of
comic and tragic elements, and Beckett's 'gift for provoca-
tion', which he felt would shake a lot of theatre people. 'I
read it without understanding it very well,' he recalled, 'but
I felt a kind of mysterious voice which shook my natural
laziness, which said it must be put on, and I must direct it.'

At the time he was working on Strindberg's difficult
play *The Ghost Sonata*. Beckett came to see the production
several times and liked what he saw, feeling Blin had faithfully followed the playwright's intentions. Blin later joked
that Beckett was impressed by the fact that the theatre was
half empty, presumably believing that a small and dedicated
band of theatregoers would provide an ideal audience for
his own work. The two men met to talk about the possibility
of a production. Finding a shared interest in the comics of
the silent screen and in Irish theatre, especially the plays of
J M Synge, they hit it off immediately, beginning a lifelong
friendship. Blin had by now also read Beckett's first play
Eleutheria. This was a more traditional work, with seven-
teen characters, elaborate props and complicated lighting,
and like *Waiting for Godot* was unperformed. Blin said it
would be impossible for him to put it on, as he was poor

and had only limited resources, but that he could stage *En attendant Godot*, since it required only four actors – who could, if necessary, wear their own clothes – and nothing more than a spotlight and a bare branch to signify a tree.

After months of trying to place the play, Beckett felt this was his last chance, and agreed to let Blin have it. Unfortunately, the managers of the Gaîté-Montparnasse were not enthusiastic about staging it. Blin then spent the best part of three years trying to find the right theatre, and raise financial backing for a production. The breakthrough came when the French government decided to offer small grants to cover the costs of the first production of new plays in French. When Blin applied for a grant, the minister for the arts, Georges Neveaux, wrote back: 'You are quite right wanting to direct *En attendant Godot*. It is an astonishing play, needless to say. I am fiercely for it.' With his key support the application was successful, although the money was only just enough to cover the actors' wages and the cost of the poster.

Even then it took a while to find a theatre willing to stage the play. An agreement was signed with the Théâtre de Poche, but the arrangement fell through. The small Théâtre de Port Chasseur did actually schedule it, but then insisted that Blin dispense with the crucial tree, which he refused to do. Finally Jean-Marie Serreau, the manager of the Théâtre Babylone and a pioneer of the French avant-garde, offered to mount the production. Serreau, well-known for his adventurous choice of new plays, was deep in debt and his theatre threatened with closure, but decided that if he was 'going to shut up shop, why not go out on a high note?' A few private individuals, including the actress Delphine Seyrig, put money into the production.

In its knockabout and comic elements *Waiting for Godot* reflected Beckett's youthful interest in the music-hall and the circus, as well as his delight in the silent-screen antics of Charlie Chaplin, Buster Keaton, Ben Turpin and Harry Langdon. In Blin's mind the ideal casting would have been Chaplin as Vladimir, Keaton as Estragon, and Charles

Laughton as Pozzo. But in reality he found the play diffi-cult to cast. Several actors turned down parts because they couldn't understand the play, or believed no one would come to see it; others accepted, but then left after further delays in finding a suitable venue. At one point Blin thought of himself for Vladimir, but eventually cast Lucien Raimbourg, an out-of-work cabaret singer and vaude-villian performer, while for Estragon he chose Pierre Latour. Several actors turned down the part of Lucky before Blin persuaded his friend Jean Martin to play it. Blin ended up playing Pozzo himself – despite Beckett's preference for having an actor who was 'a mass of flesh'.

From the beginning Beckett would reveal little about the origins of the play. He did admit to having been very struck by Caspar David Friedrich's painting 'Two Men Observing the Moon'. There was speculation that the story was partly inspired by his wartime experiences: the group for which he was working in the French resistance was betrayed, and he and Suzanne had to flee Paris and live in harsh condi-tions in the village of Rousillon in the rural south, waiting for the war to end. Another possible influence was thought to be his work after the war with the Irish Red Cross in St-Lô in Normandy, where he witnessed much devastation and misery, working among people in desperate need of food and clothing clinging on to life in a ruined landscape.

When Blin asked Beckett about the origin of the word Godot, he said that it was based on the French word meaning heavy boot, *godillot*, since boots were a feature of the play. Later Beckett enjoyed the confusion caused by the circulation of other versions. One popular one had him asking a group who were watching the Tour de France in the street what they were doing, and receiving the reply 'Nous attendons Godot', a reference to a cyclist who had not yet passed. Another, rather less plausible, had him rebuffing a Parisian prostitute on the rue Godot de Mauroy, who then asked: 'Are you waiting for Godot?' On the question of whether Godot stood for God, he pointed out that the play was written in French, where the word was *Dieu*, but admitted that the link could have been in his subconscious.

Blin had rehearsed the play for a year with various actors during the search for a theatre. Beckett sat in on most of the rehearsals, but rarely intervened directly. 'I have no ideas on the theatre, I know nothing about it,' he had confessed not long before. Blin kept to his many detailed stage directions, and encouraged the actors to stick close to the text, and not embellish it. 'I didn't want to bother the actors with metaphysical notions,' he recalled. 'I made them play the basic level, concretely.' Beckett talked discreetly to Blin at the end of the day, suggesting cuts when a piece of dialogue seemed not to work, and agreeing to small textual changes suggested by the director. Blin sometimes had difficulty in fathoming Beckett's reaction to their work, often having to rely on surreptitious glances or decoding his cryptic comments. Despite his lack of experience in the theatre, Beckett already had firm ideas about how to stage the play, favouring a stylised rather than a naturalistic type of performance, with a clear separation of speech and movement.

Blin had been struck by the circus element in the play, and the dialogue full of one-liners. He initially thought of staging it in a circus ring, with the actors coming on as clowns. But Beckett opposed the idea, arguing that too much emphasis on this aspect might distract from the play's seriousness, and that since there were visual references to vaudeville and the work of Chaplin and Keaton and Laurel and Hardy as well as to clowning, it would be too specific. Interestingly in the light of later productions, he made no reference in the text to the characters being tramps. His only demand in relation to their costumes was that all four should wear bowler hats, which gave them the appearance of members of the bourgeoisie down on their luck.

On 3 January 1953, four years after Beckett wrote it, in a converted Paris shop at the end of a cobblestone courtyard at 38 Boulevard Raspail on the Left Bank, with room for just 240 people sitting on folding chairs facing a small, angled stage which had no curtain, *Waiting for Godot* had its first performance. Word had spread that an unusual play was coming to the Babylone. Although Beckett was still relatively unknown in France, the play had recently been published, as had his novels *Molloy* and *Malone meurt*, and an abridged version of the play had been broadcast on the radio. On opening night the theatre was full to overflowing. There was however one significant absentee: Beckett's horror of such occasions prompted him to leave Paris, and to rely for an account of the performance on Suzanne. This was to become a lifelong habit: 'I see all my mistakes,' he said.

The first review in *La Libération* seemed promising, describing Beckett as 'one of today's best playwrights'. But many reviewers were baffled by the play. The most powerful of them, Jean-Jacques Gautier of *Le Figaro*, chose not to review it, while the writer Gabriel Marcel thought the play was not theatre at all. But Jacques Lemarchand was sympathetic, observing: 'To arrive at such simplicity and force, one needs an intelligence of the heart and a kind of generosity, without which talent and experience count for little.' Significantly, two of the most positive comments came from fellow-playwrights: Jean Anouilh compared the occasion in importance to the arrival of Pirandello's *Six Characters in Search of an Author*, describing it as 'the music-hall sketch of Pascal's *Pensées* as played by the Fratellini clowns', and as 'a masterpiece that will cause despair for men in general and for playwrights in particular'. Armand Salacrou wrote: 'We were waiting for this play of our time, with its new tone, its simple and modest language, and its closed circular plot... An author has appeared who has taken us by the hand to lead us into his universe.'

The play inevitably provoked controversy among its audiences, many of whom were shocked by the conversational idiom. One night there was a near riot, with insults flying around and whistles filling the auditorium, so that Blin was forced to lower the curtain before the end of the first act. There was then a confrontation with the hostile members of the audience, who eventually left, allowing the show to continue. On another occasion supporters and protesters came to blows during the interval. The play became a *succès de scandale*, and the one that it became fashionble to see. It ran for over a hundred performances at the Babylone, with people frequently being turned away. Blin briefly revived it there in the autumn, and then toured it through France, Germany, Switzerland and Italy. After struggling for years to make his name as a novelist, at the age of forty-seven Beckett had suddenly achieved fame – as a playwright.

3 Rehearsals: Week 1

Tuesday 5 July

As Peter begins rehearsing the Shaw play in the large upstairs room of the community centre, the *Waiting for Godot* company start work in the basement. It's a fairly tight acting area, with less space in the wings and at the back than the actors will have when they get to Bath. Beckett's 'low mound', on which Estragon sits at the start of the play, is represented for now by a small table. A permanent pillar of the building, though not quite in the right position, stands in for the single tree. At the back of the playing area, as if playing truant from a production of *Endgame*, is a black plastic dustbin. Sitting at two narrow tables in front of the actors are Cordelia Monsey and assistant stage manager Donna Reeves. I perch in the corner, hoping to be an unobtrusive observer.

This morning James Laurenson (Vladimir) and Alan Dobie (Estragon) are working on the first section of the play. Cordelia's brief is to use the annotated script of Peter's 1997 and 1998 production as a basis of blocking the new one, but to be open to changes that the actors might want to make. 'Feel free to move around the room,' she says. 'Some of this is a movable feast.' This sometimes proves complicated, since Alan remembers the moves from 1998, while James is coming fresh to the text; and while Alan is already off the book, James is inevitably not yet sure of his lines. 'I need to nail down what you did before, so we can then see if it still works,' he says.

Alan demonstrates some of the moves to him, and they quickly establish a good jokey relationship as they work through the opening ten pages. James is the taller of the two, mercurial and self-deprecating; Alan, squat and trim, with a white beard and sporting a sun hat, is more watchful, but full of imaginative ideas. The two of them enjoy an early discussion about the numerous pauses and silences that Beckett demands in his stage direction. The repartee flows:

ALAN: Is this a pause, a silence or a long silence?
CORDELIA: It's a silence.
JAMES: 'What did you do at work today, Dad?' – 'I observed a silence.'
ALAN: What a profession!
JAMES: Can we do that silence again?

Cordelia is keen for the actors to stick from the start to the exact words of the text. Donna is marking her script with any deviations they make, and in a pause she goes through these with them. They then run through the early exchanges with a little more confidence.

After lunch they are joined by Terence Rigby (Pozzo) and Richard Dormer (Lucky). Their first entry, with Pozzo driving Lucky across the stage, is a formidable logistic challenge. Richard, with a heavy rope round his neck, has to carry a big suitcase, a picnic basket, a stool, and Terence's jacket. He and Terence, who cracks the whip with convincing relish, have to make sure the rope is taut and slack at the right moments, a demand made more difficult by the fact that the stage right exit ends abruptly at the basement window. The entry proves a nightmare, and will clearly demand a lot of practice.

Terence looks like an excellent choice for Pozzo, his strong brooding presence and general quietness combining to produce an air of mystery as well as a sense of danger. Richard, eager and chatty, the youngest in the cast and the only Irishman, has no inhibitions in immediately testing himself physically, simulating Lucky's pain and suffering to impressive effect.

Like Alan, Terence is a veteran of the 1998 production, and is generally keen to stick to the moves he had then. But occasionally his memory of them is in conflict with that of Cordelia, who assisted Peter on that production, and has made a point of watching the video the previous night.

Alan, meanwhile, has a different concern. 'Having missed out on those two weeks when we would normally have the book in our hands, we need to hear the stage directions.'

It's been essentially a practical day, with little time to explore motive or meaning, though in passing Cordelia tosses one theory into the pool: 'Has Vladimir invented Godot? I think there's scope for a big discussion there.'

As the actors break for the day, I ask Alan Dobie what attracts him to the play.

> The exciting thing is that it's one of those plays that has a lot of metaphor in it. It's not just a narrative, so you can play it on many levels. It's also a very physical play, it's got clowning and music hall and end-of-the-pier stuff in it, so it's got a nostalgic value, especially if you remember those things from your youth, which I do. They've always rather appealed to me, those kind of characters.

> I always wanted to play Vladimir, but I got offered Estragon. Vladimir is the pivot, the one who steers it along, while Estragon is in his wake. Vladimir is the hopeful one, always looking forward to the future, while Estragon is the negative, despairing one. They're both trapped in a world they can't quite make sense of, like we all are. Vladimir is hopeful, but doubts whether there is any purpose to his life, though he hopes to discover the solution eventually. He lives in hope but fears he might be wrong, while Estragon is the opposite, he plays the game of life and fears he may be right, that there is nothing else. So it's a good combination, a good balancing act between the two of them.

> As an actor all you can do is play the text, try and bring it to life. I don't think there's any point in trying to put over any interpretations you may have read about. If it's a well-written play it comes out anyway. With this play, most of the interpretation is not what we do with it, but how the audience reads it, and what they receive. As T S Eliot said, I hope the audience get more out of my plays than I put into them. Picasso said something similar, he said, I never finish a painting, I expect each member of the public who looks at it

to finish it themselves. We have to let the audience put their own interpretation on it rather than putting a blanket one on it for them.

While we're working with Cordelia we have to try and remember as much of the last production as we can. Terry and I have done it before, so we can get a basic skeleton there, and Peter can re-work it when he comes in. I imagine James might want me to stop telling him what we did before, but he doesn't seem to object.

Thursday 7 July

I arrive to find Peter and the actors from both companies gathered grim-faced round the radio. News is coming through of problems in the centre of London, apparently explosions on the underground, though no one quite knows the cause. Anxiously people try to make calls on their mobiles, but fail: frighteningly, the whole network seems to be shut down. Once it becomes clear that there are bombs involved, Peter decides to cancel the Shaw rehearsals. Terence and Richard are not called today, so Cordelia asks Alan and James if they want to carry on rehearsing. They do, so we troop sombrely down to the basement.

The work is now focused on Act 2. The actors are into a section which underlines how much Vladimir and Estragon are dependent on each other. During the morning various questions are briefly raised: To what extent is Godot a figment of Vladimir's imagination? Has he simply invented Godot to keep Estragon with him? If so, has he set up the Boy? And why does the Boy address Estragon as Mr Albert? But at this moment there's little inclination to explore such questions, so they concentrate on more practical matters relating to the text and the moves.

James now has a hat and an authentically threadbare coat, while Alan has exchanged his sun hat for a small bowler, which makes him look even more pugnacious than before. This enables them to try for the first time the moment where they exchange hats several times. It's an old music-hall routine, used by the Marx Brothers in their film *Duck Soup* and with roots in the *commedia dell'arte*. It will be amusing when it works, which it doesn't yet.

During the morning everyone has left their mobiles on, in the hope that the network will be re-connected, so families and friends will be able to make contact to ensure they are not affected by the bombings. So the morning is occasionally interrupted by ring tones. Despite this, and the uncertainty about what is going on elsewhere in London, the two actors manage to keep their concentration in impressive fashion.

After lunch they work on some of the other music-hall routines. Their timing is developing fast. An exchange with a carrot and a radish is already quite polished, and the leg joke in the style of Harpo Marx is delightfully deft. Even the silences, notably those between the talk about 'all the dead voices', are becoming more precise.

Some of their own exchanges are becoming positively Beckettian.

> JAMES: (*As they stumble inexpertly through their waltz.*)
>   Who exactly is leading?
> ALAN: I don't know.

The physical elements of the play are beginning to take shape, and the actors are beginning to relax into the process. After rehearsal James and I repair to the nearby pavement café, to talk about his approach to the part of Vladimir.

> I have played Vladimir before, but many moons ago, at university in New Zealand in 1961. It was directed by this rather High Church Anglican woman, who saw the play almost as a Christian tract. I don't think that's what the play's about, but that's how she saw it. I was overwhelmed by it then, so it's lovely to come back to it now.
>
> Vladimir finishes up as the only person in the world with any notion of time, which is terrifying. So he has to be set up to go to there. He's an optimist, but things constantly arrive

that dent his optimism. So his happiness is pretty fragile. I'm playing catch up of course, as I wasn't in Peter's previous production. So it's a slightly different experience at the start of rehearsals. But because Alan and Terry have hacked it before, we're able to make short cuts, which is very useful. Alan is a joy, he'll make suggestions that are spot on. If you and the actor playing Estragon are not getting on together, you can forget it. But Alan is terrific.

I learnt as much of the part as possible before we came to rehearsal. The last three plays I've done with Peter he's insisted on that. It was quite an effort, because the play is so dense and detailed. Some actors don't like to do that, but I've found it a useful practice here. Once you have the text in your head, you can move on more easily to the movements that the stage directions require, and then to the pauses and silences, all of which go to make up the music and rhythm of the play, like a detailed musical score.

So I'm coming at it from that point of view, rather than through any great philosophical or religious meaning. If you're telling the story, I think you have to put interpretations to one side at first. There's a lot of things you can't pin down, at least certainly not in the early days of rehearsals. The text and stage directions are very precise, so it's good to begin there, you need some kind of armature to start a play with. Some actors would find blocking it straight away inhibiting, but if it's a good play, it's not. It gives you a structure to work with. You can change such a lot at a later stage, between the technical rehearsal and the press night, as long as the groundwork is good.

Friday 8 July

Because of the chaos caused to London's transport system by yesterday's bombs, today is a shortened rehearsal, devoted to the Vladimir and Estragon section that follows Pozzo and Lucky's exit in Act 1.

James is virtually off the book now, and the quick-fire exchanges are getting up to speed. But the constant repetition of certain phrases ('What are we waiting for?' 'What do we do now?' 'Shall we go?') are still causing him and Alan considerable difficulty, leading to further Godotesque exchanges:

> JAMES: What do I say here?
> DONNA: I'm not sure where we are.
> JAMES: Nor am I.

They're still struggling, prompted by Donna, to get Beckett's text precisely as he wrote it. But the work on the music-hall routines is noticeably sharper. They practise the hat-lifting routine in their synchronised farewells to Pozzo and Lucky, trying to get the right musical gradations in the various 'Adieus'. Cordelia offers to show them a DVD of Laurel and Hardy which Richard has requested, but Alan says he'd rather not watch anyone else for the moment.

'Wonderful, and desperately sad,' Cordelia observes, as they reach the final moment of the act ('Well, shall we go? Yes, let's go. *They do not move.*'). James and Alan then attempt to run through all the sections they've worked on this week. It's still fairly ragged, but the rapport between the two of them is a good one.

Under Cordelia's detailed guidance it's been a useful foundation-laying week. Over tea she talks about her role in the production.

> I'm really acting as what used to be called the stage direc-
> tor: getting the actors to remember the staging, and to stay
> as close as possible to the text. Of course it's not going to
> be an identical copy of the previous production, not least
> because we have two new actors. But already they seem to
> be working well with the two who've done it before. That's
> especially important with Vladimir and Estragon: happily,
> James has been very keen on the suggestions Alan has been
> making and, in the case of the touches from old music-hall
> acts, happy literally to fall into step with him. The partner-
> ship between Richard and Terence is also clearly one of
> mutual respect and admiration. So it's been a creative time.

own English translation. The UK rights were secured jointly by the West End theatre manager Donald Albery and the director Peter Glenville. Encouraged by friends, including Margot Fonteyn and Dorothy Tutin, who read the play and supported the idea of staging it, they attempted to cast it, hoping to find at least one and preferably two West End stars willing to appear in it. It is now part of the mythology that the two main roles were quickly turned down by John Gielgud, Michael Hordern, Alec Guinness and Ralph Richardson. The reality was more complicated. Hordern certainly turned it down, saying he didn't understand the script. There is no definite evidence that Gielgud was offered it, but he certainly made it clear that he loathed it, finding it sordid and pessimistic – though later he admitted it contained some good writing. Guinness, according to one second-hand account, disliked the idea of playing Estragon, but Beckett's authorised biographer James Knowlson, who interviewed him, says he was keen to play the part, and remained enthusiastic for some time, only being finally prevented from doing so by other commitments.

Richardson, who was appearing with Gielgud at the Haymarket in *A Day by the Sea*, was bemused by the script, but interested, and sought the advice of other cast members. Gielgud told him it was rubbish, but Irene Worth said he would be mad not to do it. In October 1954, during a brief trip to London, Beckett came to Richardson's dressing-room at the Haymarket. Richardson told him that he liked the play on the whole, but that he had a number of questions ('I had a little laundry list'), the first being, Who is Pozzo? Beckett, who from the start had refused to answer all such questions, told him that everything he knew about Pozzo was in the text, and that the same applied to the other characters. He also explained that, if by Godot he had meant to indicate God, he would have said God. Despite this obviously unsatisfactory meeting on both sides, Richardson, according to Albery, continued to be in the frame, and there was even talk that he and Guinness would take the production to New York after a London run. In the end Richardson turned it down because of other commitments, later describing doing so as 'one of the greatest mistakes of my life'.

The play had also been read by the agent Peggy Ramsay, who was enthralled by it. Although she didn't represent Beckett, according to her biographer Colin Chambers she campaigned on his behalf. She sent a copy of the play to the Arts Council's drama officer, who sent a rude letter back, describing it as 'drivel'. Meanwhile Albery and Glenville tried other alternatives, including Oscar Lewenstein, who wanted to produce it with the playwright Ronald Duncan, but also found that leading actors were not prepared to risk playing in it. Beckett, who was opposed to what he called this 'star chasing', became increasingly impatient, arguing that if the play couldn't be performed with a normal decent set of actors and a competent director, then it wasn't worth doing at all.

A further obstacle was the continuing existence of the theatre censor, the Lord Chamberlain, without whose licence of approval no play could be performed on the stage. This ludicrous and destructive institution, left over from the nineteenth century, was not to be abolished until 1968. The last bastion of a genteel moral code that had vanished decades before, the Lord Chamberlain specialised in objecting to any reference that was remotely sexual or lavatorial. He appears to have had a special prejudice against French plays, having not long before refused a licence to Sartre's *Huis Clos* – even if it was performed in French.

In the case of *Waiting for Godot* he made objections to a dozen passages, which Beckett thought preposterous, and initially refused to countenance. Among the more ludicrous demands, the word 'piss' would have to be changed to 'piddle', and 'the privates' become 'the guts'. The impasse looked set to torpedo the whole production. Eventually Beckett agreed to a few minor changes – such as changing 'crap' to 'warts', and 'Fartov' to 'Popov'. But he refused to budge on the more substantial ones, which included Vladimir and Estragon's discussion about whether hanging themselves would bring on an erection; the first fifteen lines of Lucky's long speech; several lines containing references to Christ and the crucifixion; and the final moment when Estragon's trousers fall down. A special reading of the play in the New theatre, arranged for the benefit of an official from the Lord Chamberlain's office, and with Dorothy Tutin reading the Boy, failed to bring any change in the situation. The production seemed doomed.

Albery eventually got round these two problems by abandoning his pursuit of West End stars and, with Peter Glenville now working in America, sending the play to Peter Hall at the Arts, which as a private theatre club was not subject to the Lord Chamberlain's bizarre proscriptions. Hall, who had a keen interest in world drama and avant-garde theatre, had just directed the first production in English of Eugène Ionesco's *The Lesson*, and Julien Green's *South*. He was rehearsing his next production, Eugene O'Neill's epic *Mourning Becomes Electra*, when the script of *Waiting for Godot* arrived. Albery had been impressed by his work on *South*, and asked if he might like to put Beckett's play on at the Arts.

Hall read the script during a lengthy meal-break in the technical rehearsals for O'Neill's play. In a radio interview six years later, he remembered his first reaction to it: 'I must admit I didn't really know all of *Godot*, and I couldn't say in precise or literal terms that I understood it. But then I don't think one can say about this kind of writing or this kind of play that there is a literal or final meaning… I was immediately struck by the enormous humanity and universality of the subject, and also by the extraordinary rhythms of the writing. It was these rhythms and the almost musical flexibility of the lyricism that communicated itself to me.'

There were still casting problems, notably when Cyril Cusack turned down the chance to return to the West End and play Vladimir. 'I had terrible trouble casting it, because no one would be in it,' Hall recalls. Finally a very mixed company was assembled. Paul Daneman, a talented young member of the Old Vic who had recently won plaudits for his Justice Shallow in *Henry IV Part II*, was the original choice for Estragon, but switched to Vladimir when Cusack declined the part; Pozzo was to be played by Peter Bull, a witty, camp and eccentric actor who was later to become famous for his collection of teddy bears; Lucky was taken on by Timothy Bateson, who had recently played Osric in *Hamlet* and Trinculo in *The Tempest* at the Old Vic. The riskiest piece of casting, which turned out to be an inspired choice, was for Estragon. Peter Woodthorpe was a second-year biochemistry student at Cambridge, where Hall had been greatly impressed by his King Lear. 'I wasn't long out of Cambridge myself, so I was under the apprehension that people from the Marlowe Society, the main university company, could go straight into the professional theatre. But Peter was very good, a natural actor.'

Fifty years on, Bateson recalls his first reading of the script: 'My reaction was one of disbelief. There had never been a play quite like this before. Plays didn't start like this, they started with a white telephone and a butler saying, Her Ladyship's in the garden, she'll be in for tea directly, and I'll get her to call you back. I honestly thought it was a joke that Peter was playing on us, but he assured me it wasn't.' Peter Bull was equally baffled when he read the play: 'I thought either the author or I must be potty,' he wrote in his memoirs. 'I could not begin to understand what my proposed role meant, and decided to turn it down, as I considered it pointless to contemplate playing a part through which I could see no daylight.' However, Hall persuaded him to reconsider, arguing that he was ideal for the part; but even while accepting it, Bull played safe by insisting on a clause in his contract that allowed him to leave after a few days if he was unhappy.

Because of the play's difficulty, Hall insisted on seven weeks' rehearsal rather than the usual four. He and the actors began work on it on the top floor of the Arts on a hot day in early July. Bull remembers Hall announcing: 'I haven't really the foggiest idea what some of it means, but if we stop and discuss every line, we'll never open. I think it may be dramatically effective, but there's no hope of finding out till the first night.' In 1961 Hall himself remembered the start of rehearsals. 'The play was so difficult – we didn't understand it – that we absolutely had to pull together. Perhaps it's a help to a director when a play is obscure. The actors can't have their own pet theories or argue too much. Mine didn't anyway. They trusted me, and off we went.'

One fundamental question needed to be settled early on: Were the characters clowns or tramps? Beckett himself gave no indication; for the original Paris production he merely stipulated that all four characters should wear bowler hats. So on that occasion there was a clown element, but also a sense of the characters being members of the bourgeoisie fallen on hard times. At the beginning of rehearsals at the Arts, Hall announced that Vladimir and Estragon were clowns. But as he worked on the text with the actors the characters soon began to emerge as tramps – which is how they would generally be played for the next half-century. Hall remembers now that, 'It was very difficult, because most of the actors thought it was a load of balls. They worked hard, but sometimes they thought they were in a kind of con job, that the play was a suit of Emperor's New Clothes. But once they started to get their tongues round those cadences, they began to recognise they were working on a major writer.'

David Collison, the assistant stage manager, recalls: 'During rehearsals I and the rest of the stage management were very puzzled by the play, and so were the actors. But then we all got slightly hooked on it.' Bateson recalls: 'In rehearsals we didn't discuss meanings, because we didn't have to: it just worked. Peter used to say to us, Whatever it's all about, whatever our understanding of the play, we must engage the audience, they must be sitting there saying to themselves, There but for the grace of God go I.' But he also remembers Bull struggling with Pozzo: 'One day he got rather a complicated note from Peter about how he should say a line. When he tried it and still couldn't get it right, he stamped his foot and said: "Oh, get Elwyn Brooke-Jones to play the part!"' Bull himself, who was hostile to the play, admitted he could make no sense of Pozzo's character until the last week of rehearsals, when, bizarrely, he 'suddenly decided to cheat and pretend Miss Margaret Rutherford was playing the role, which had the immediate and blessed effect of stopping embarrassing myself'.

One of the main difficulties facing the actors was the constant repetition of certain phrases, which made learning the lines extremely difficult. Another was Beckett's insistence on precisely timed pauses and silences, some of which the actors feared might make it appear they had forgotten their lines. Hall insisted they should follow the playwright's instructions: 'It's a bizarre play, and we might as well play it bizarrely,' Daneman recalled him saying. Bateson remembers that 'Peter was very good at disciplining us and saying, Just let Sam do the work for you.' Beckett himself declined to come to London, but Hall spoke to him on the phone, and corresponded with him. 'Sadly the letters have disappeared, destroyed in a fire,' he says. 'The main burden of them was that you should trust the text and allow the play to say what it says, and if you don't know what it says, don't try and put something else on it. I think he believed, with a certain amount of reason, that if you trust the silences and the pauses the text will start to tell you what it's about.'

By the end of rehearsals the actors had, according to Daneman, 'a fairly good idea of the play, but no sense of the weight of it'. Expectations about its reception were low: according to Bateson, 'We knew we were in for a failure, none of us thought it was going to do anything.' Collison recalls: 'Peter gave the actors a pep talk, saying that they had to hold the pauses and stay in character, even if people shouted out during them.' The first night audience in the 350-seat theatre seemed to confirm their worst fears: there were, Hall remembers, yawns, mock snores and some barracking. 'Later on the audience nearly erupted into open hostility, but then decided not to bother and settled instead into still, glum boredom.' Bull felt the actors should have been given medals for gallantry, as 'waves of hostility came whirling over the footlights'. The performance on the small, cramped stage was punctuated by audible groans and the sound of upturned seats. When Estragon said, 'Nothing happens, nobody comes, nobody goes, it's awful,' a very upper-class voice called out from the audience, 'Hear, hear.' The critic Harold Hobson later recalled the atmosphere: 'Certain lines in the play, such as "I've been better entertained," were received with ironical laughter and applause; and when one of the characters yawned, the yawn was echoed and amplified by a humorist in the stalls.' At the end there was mild applause, cheers and counter cheers. 'A depression and sense of anti-climax descended on us all,' Bull recalled.

The critics attending that historic first night were generally as bemused as the actors initially had been. Yet the majority of their notices were not quite as harsh as some later accounts have suggested. Some were certainly brutally dismissive, notably Bernard Levin's, who asserted in *Truth* that Beckett had written 'a really remarkable piece of twaddle...remarkable not for its content, which is nil, but for the fact that with it he has managed to take for a simultaneous ride both the professional lowbrows and the professional highbrows.' Cecil Wilson's review in the *Daily Mail* was equally scathing: 'The play comes to us with a great reputation among the intelligentsia of Paris. And so far as I am concerned, the intelligentsia of Paris may have it back as soon as they wish.' The critic of the *Star* called it 'poppycock', while W A Darlington of the *Daily Telegraph* thought it was 'as odd a piece of playwriting as you could wish to see... It is superb as a serious frolic for highbrows, but in the regular work-a-day theatre it has no place at all. No management would ask the ordinary playgoer to face it.' Meanwhile Milton Schulman in the *Evening Standard* called it 'another of those plays that tries to lift superficiality to significance through obscurity. Beckett's symbols are seldom more demanding than a nursery version of *The Pilgrim's Progress*.'

Philip Hope-Wallace in the *Guardian* thought the language 'flat and feeble in the extreme', and called it 'a play to send the rationalist out of his mind, and induce tooth-gnashing among people who would take Lewis Carroll's Red Queen and Edward Lear's nonsense exchanges as the easiest stuff in the world'. But Arthur Cookman, writing anonymously in *The Times*, was less harsh: while suggesting that Beckett's 'patently elemental personages are figments in whom we cannot ultimately believe since they lack universality', he also wrote that Beckett 'possesses the dramatic instinct in a most original sense', and that the play 'holds the stage most wittily'. There was widespread praise for Hall's production, and the actors' performances. Nevertheless the first generally negative critical and public response suggested the play would have to close in a matter of days. But the situation changed dramatically the following Sunday when Kenneth Tynan and Harold Hobson, the two most influential and heavyweight critics, came out in support of the play.

In his characteristically stylish and provocative review, Tynan immediately identified the play's revolutionary potential: 'By all the known criteria, Samuel Beckett's *Waiting for Godot* is a dramatic vacuum,' he wrote in the *Observer*. 'It has no plot, no climax, no denouement; no beginning, no middle, no end… It frankly jettisons everything by which we recognise theatre. It arrives at the custom-house, as it were, with no luggage, no passport, and nothing to declare; yet it gets through, as might a pilgrim from Mars. It does this, I believe, by appealing to a definition of drama much more fundamental than any in the books. A play, it asserts and proves, is basically a means of spending two hours in the dark without being bored… It forced me to examine the rules which have hitherto governed the drama; and, having done so, to pronounce them not elastic enough. It is validly new: and hence I declare myself, as the Spanish would say, *godotista*.'

Harold Hobson's review for the *Sunday Times* was also mainly positive, though it might have been less so had it not been for an encounter he had with Peggy Ramsay during the interval of the first performance. Known for his passion for and knowledge of the theatre in France, Hobson appeared to Ramsay to be depressed: apparently he wanted to write a positive review, but thought the play very peculiar, and hadn't enjoyed it. Ramsay argued its merits, believing it to be an important work, and telling Hobson he had a reputation to maintain as a perceptive critic of French drama. The next day, when she and Hall discussed the notices in the daily papers, she suggested Hobson might be encouraged to be more positive if a copy of Beckett's novel *Watt* was sent to him, and this was duly done.

In his review Hobson still expressed his reservations about the play, suggesting that trying to capture its essence was like 'trying to catch Leviathan in a butterfly net'. He felt that Beckett had 'got it all wrong', but 'in a tremendous way'. He had mixed feelings about the cross-talk dialogue between Vladimir and Estragon: 'It is bewildering. It is exasperating. It is insidiously exciting.' But he ended with a ringing declaration: 'Go and see *Waiting for Godot*. At the worst you will discover a curiosity, a four-leaf clover, a black tulip; at the best, something that will lodge in a corner of your mind for as long as you live.'

The effect of these two notices was no less than sensational. The theatre was immediately full, and remained so for the rest of its four-week run at the Arts. In September the play transferred to the Criterion in the heart of the West End, where it ran for over six months, and then toured the country for a further eight weeks. Contrary to legend, it was not just Tynan and Hobson who lavished praise on the play and turned it into a success. The *Spectator* critic called it a 'fascinating tragic-comedy, a unique play that triumphs over all our ideas of what drama should be', while Richard Findlater in *Tribune* praised 'a work of rare theatrical excitement...which enlarges so memorably the frontiers of our theatre'. But Tynan and Hobson helped further by following up their reviews the next Sunday. Tynan wrote: 'It will be a conversational necessity for many years to have seen *Waiting for Godot*.' Hobson, having now evidently read *Watt*, observed: 'The linguistic architecture of *Waiting for Godot* is of a high and subtle kind', and added, 'I am not sure that Mr Samuel Beckett is not the profoundest of living humorists: yet comparatively few people seem to be aware that he is a humorist at all.' He ended: '*Waiting for Godot* is one of the four funniest entertainments in London.'

The play frequently provoked negative reactions, and occasional outbursts from the audience. One night at the Criterion, when the actors reached Estragon's line 'What do we do now, now that we are happy?', a voice cried out: 'I'm not happy, I've never been so bored in all my life.' Hugh Burden, who had taken over from Daneman as Vladimir, quickly responded: 'I think that was Godot.' The production also produced strong reactions within the theatre world. Alec McCowen, later to play Vladimir, recalls disliking it intensely: 'I was quite horrified by it, and tried to leave in the interval.' Playwright Ronald Harwood was alarmed for a different reason: 'I was terribly frightened when I first saw it, because I thought, Maybe there's nothing, this is it – and that's a terrible realisation.' But another future Vladimir, Julian Glover, was stirred in a different way: 'For my generation the play was a complete surprise, totally out of left field. I went with Eileen Atkins, my first wife, and we were absolutely staggered by it. We reeled out thinking, Where is the theatre going now?' 'Most exciting evening I've spent in the theatre for a very long time,' John Osborne wrote to his agent. 'It made me do a lot of thinking.'

The play quickly entered the general consciousness. When the new non-parking signs appeared in the street, a *Punch* cartoon joked 'No waiting – not even for Godot', while on New Year's Eve a BBC announcer, looking across Piccadilly Circus to the Criterion, said: 'Up here we're all waiting for 1956, while down there they're all waiting for Godot.' It was also extensively debated in the press and on television. In the *Times Literary Supplement* there was a lengthy correspondence about its meaning, centring on whether it was a modern morality play on Christian themes or an Existentialist play, or neither. It also provoked strong views amongst other playwrights. Sean O'Casey, writing in *Encore* magazine, was particularly savage on his fellow-Irishman: 'This Beckett is a clever writer, and that he has written a rotting and remarkable play there is no doubt; but his philosophy isn't my philosophy, for within him there is no hazard of hope; no desire for it; nothing in it but a lust for despair, and a crying of woe, not in a wilderness, but in a garden.'

The play's controversial success prompted the BBC to think again about its earlier dismissal of the play as 'phoney'. A report on the original production from its Paris representative had judged it to be 'extraordinarily effective', but concluded that 'it ceased to be effective after we had a drink at the interval'. The arrival of the script at the BBC's Drama Department prompted some discussion about how it might be treated. One producer asked: 'Is one to think of Jimmy Edwards and Dick Bentley, or Tommy Handley or Deryck Guyler, or two actors with comedian talent, but intellectual background?' But the head of drama Val Gielgud, well known for his aversion to experiment, felt it was 'basically phoney', as did the producer Donald McWhinnie (who later became a great champion of Beckett, both on the radio and in the theatre). The project was dropped, but once the play opened in London, the BBC did a *volte-face*. On Gielgud's instruction the producer Raymond Raikes went to see the play at the Criterion, and concluded that it would be highly suitable for radio, and with the same cast. 'His small company has been brilliantly directed by Peter Hall, and his direction extends to a studied control of the dialogue, with its extraordinary contrasts of rhythms and its compelling climaxes,' he reported, ending: 'May I suggest we record and broadcast this production as soon as possible, lest it be said that the BBC has once again "missed the boat".'

In contrast to later productions, Hall's was relatively naturalistic in style. Vladimir and Estragon were portrayed realistically, and Pozzo was recognisably an Irish upper-class landowner. The set, designed by Peter Snow, was visually more elaborate than the Paris production: a raised bank at the back sprouted various bits of vegetation, the lone tree was fringed by beds of reeds, while at the front of the stage by the low mound was a tar barrel, a rock and several pieces of stone. 'There was too much scenery, the set was a bit too busy,' Hall says now. 'I didn't understand then that less was more.' He had also used short pieces of music before and during the action to create atmosphere. According to Collison, who worked on the sound, they included an ethereal air for the entry of the Boy, and fragments that began whenever Lucky moved, and ended when he stopped. 'The wisps of music were bits of Bartok, very light, very delicate – and very wrong,' Hall remembers. 'I blush to think of them now, but I was journeying in a new country and finding my way.'

At the end of the year Beckett came over from Paris to see the production at the Criterion. This time, to his disgust, the cuts demanded by the Lord Chamberlain had to be made, because the performance was now in a public theatre. Beckett was rarely satisfied with a production, and Hall's was no exception. Hall remembers Beckett saying to him: 'It's fine, but you don't bore the audience enough. Make them wait longer. Make the pauses longer. You should bore them.' According to Alan Schneider, who saw the play with Beckett on five successive nights, he was worried about what he saw as a sentimental element, and would have preferred a harsher simplicity. He was later reported not to like the production's 'cluttered stage, and pauses which were not long enough, and which were, to make matters worse, filled with heavenly music'.

Beckett was to become famous, or notorious, for his refusal to provide any explanation about the play or its characters. 'I know no more about the characters than what they say, what they do, and what happens to them,'

5 Rehearsals: Week 2

Monday 11 July

Before rehearsals begin I ask Peter what made him choose these particular actors for his new production.

Alan Dobie is one of the best actors around, though I don't think that's recognised. He has enormous comic energy, he can be very moving without being sentimental, and that's very important for Estragon. It's a very dangerous part, because it can very easily become sentimental. Alan has a steely quality about him, but he also has a quality of vulnerability, which is right for the part.

James Laurenson is one of my favourite actors: there are few who can express the thinking man more accessibly. Vladimir is in a sense the scholar, the thinker, the priest, the intellectual, and James is just right for that: he's very quick, he has a very alert mind and, most importantly, he's clearly a good pairing with Alan.

Terence Rigby I've worked with many times before, including the original productions of Pinter's *The Homecoming* and *No Man's Land*. There's a danger about him, a brutality, yet I think he makes enormous sense of his character. Pozzo is a very haunted character, a man on the brink of disintegration, and Terence knows all about that.

I saw Richard Dormer in his play last year about Hurricane Higgins. It was a wonderful piece of playwriting, a wonderful piece of direction by his wife, but most of all a wonderful performance. His verbal dexterity and an extraordinary physical ability made me think he would be ideal for Lucky. I think he's a great actor in the making.

The rehearsal starts with Peter suggesting that James and Alan run the text without interruption as far as the first entrance of Pozzo and Lucky, to show him how it's shaping up after their first week's groundwork. They do so, after which he says: 'I think it's fantastically crisp and slick, and very fluent. But it's lacking in sub-text. You're not living the pauses and they're not long enough. You need to find the sense of waiting to show time passing. So now we need to take it to pieces, and put it together again. It needs framing.'

Close textual analysis is now the order of the day, as they move slowly through the first section. 'What a lot of non-sequiturs!' Alan observes. Peter likens the relationship between Vladimir and Lucky to that of an old married couple: 'When Estragon says, Not now, it's like a wife saying, Not tonight dear.' He encourages James and Alan to recognise a new thought, or a change of mood during their arguments. 'I'm on my high horse here,' Alan suggests. 'Not as high as mine,' James counters.

They stop frequently to examine some of the more enigmatic lines, as for example the reference to Estragon being beaten. 'It's probably a fictitious story that I come back with every morning,' Alan suggests, and Peter agrees. They take a while to decide whether Vladimir is more worried about the contents of his hat or his bladder. Alan wants to know if a certain line should be addressed to the audience. 'We'll probably find many examples of this,' Peter observes. 'We haven't done it in other productions, because Sam didn't want it. But let's try it.'

In the afternoon, joined by Terence and Richard, they jump over to Act 2. Terence now has his Anglo-Irish country gentleman's waistcoat and boots, and is becoming more forbidding by the moment: his full-blooded cry of 'Pity! Pity!' as he lies on the floor is hair-raising. Richard is still in jeans, but from the beginning he adopts Lucky's desperate downtrodden demeanour, expressing vividly his physical and mental agony. Choreographing Pozzo and Lucky's fall, and making sure that Terence doesn't squash Richard, proves to be a tricky manoeuvre. Alan demonstrates one way, and breaks his glasses in the process. One of the difficulties for Terence is the length of time he has to remain on the ground, emitting only an occasional cry for help, while Vladimir and Estragon endlessly discuss what to do.

Throughout, Peter keeps a very sharp eye on the pauses and silences, sticking closely to Beckett's stage directions, but ensuring that in each case the actors know why he's put them there. The mood is serious, but amicable, with Peter and the actors already establishing a good, collaborative relationship.

At the end of the day, in the small courtyard outside the rehearsal room, Richard talks to me about the challenge of playing Lucky, and about learning his epic speech.

> I read the play when I was at RADA, fifteen years ago, and saw a production more recently at the Lyric in Belfast. I was surprised at how moving it was, and how funny. Now, watching Alan and James, I'm seeing so much more in it than I saw in Belfast. I was in Crete on holiday with my wife just before rehearsals, and because Peter wanted us off the book when we started, I read the big speech again and again and again, it seemed like a thousand times. Then I started to go over the rhythm of it, and try and find images in it. But I didn't want to bring too much to it then, I wanted to colour it in the rehearsal room. It's like a piece of music, a piece of jazz because it's so discordant, but there is a rhythm in it, and a theme that runs through it, so it's like trying to learn a very, very difficult piece of music.
>
> It's when I see an image in it, like the skull in Connemara, that it works best for me. I'm coming to it as an Irishman, and I think Beckett was coming to terms with his Irish identity. He was removed from it living in France, but he was writing about the Irish. I think Lucky is in a way the voice of his mind. Lucky is remembering the famine in Ireland, but Beckett's done it very cleverly, because he doesn't actually say that it's that. He talks about the skull, and the round figures stark naked in the stockinged feet in Connemara – which was where hundreds of thousands of people died alone during the famine, all trying to get on the ships to go to America. I think that's where Beckett was coming

from, remembering that horrible moment in British and Irish history, which we all try to forget, but it's there, and that's what Lucky keeps coming back to.

I knew it would be tiring rehearsing the part, but it's proving to be exhausting. But I like to get straight in there, because the rehearsals are like a workout. In four weeks' time I'll have to do it on stage, so I want to get the hard chore over now, and get my body equipped to be able to push myself that far. I'm doing this shivering with my whole body, caused by the sheer tension of Lucky having to hold himself up on his own two feet. He's almost like Atlas, he's carrying the world on his shoulders. I think it's all there in the text, that he's gasping, he's puffing like a grampus, he's slavering, his eyes are bubbling – he's a man at death's door.

Wednesday 13 July

Before rehearsals begin there's a production meeting in the main room upstairs, attended by Peter, the production team and the designers. It's a chance to chart progress, and identify problems.

Peter has asked for a real stone for the 'low mound' Beckett describes in his stage direction. Kevin reports he has found the perfect one in the Forest of Dean, with just room enough for two to sit on it. There's a discussion about the right kind of leaves to go on the tree in Act 2: should they be new or mature growth? And what kind of chicken piece would be most appropriate for Terence to eat? The actors are keen to have the correct length of rope for Pozzo and Lucky as soon as possible; and it's agreed that Richard needs a harness to stop the rope from strangling him. Terence's stool, which gets kicked around, is in need of reinforcing. Meanwhile costume fittings are being organised, and in general the production seems up to speed.

Back in the basement, where Cordelia and company have recently completed a first run-through of the play, the photographer Nobby Clark is taking photographs, for use by the press and the theatre in Bath. Taking shots from all angles as the actors rehearse and Peter directs, he's as discreet as it's possible to be in such a small room.

Today it's Act 1 again, and the scene with Pozzo and Lucky. Terence is a commanding presence, and quite terrifying with his whip; when he's on he dominates the action. Richard once again maintains his exhausted face throughout, looking, as Estragon notes, 'on his last gasp'. Suddenly he asks: 'What age is Lucky? Or is he any age?' Peter: 'He's probably in his forties or fifties, but he hasn't got long to go.'

Richard performs the 'Think', as Lucky's long speech is called. He is now impressively word perfect. Peter suggests the way forward: 'The lyrical colours are much better now, but it needs more shape to it. I feel that Lucky is desperate to achieve coherence. I feel he has a bank of a thousand words, which he wants to plug into, but can't.' The actors try to find a way for Vladimir and Estragon to pick Lucky up when he falls at the end of the speech. 'It needs to be less naturalistic, more presentational, like the music-hall routines you do elsewhere,' Peter suggests. Alan demonstrates a particular technique, which works, and is adopted.

At one moment a mobile goes off in the middle of a silence. Could it be Godot? Eventually it's tracked down to Terence's jacket pocket. After rehearsals he and I talk over coffee about the challenge of his role.

I enjoy playing the part, I've always enjoyed having a shot at it. I think I'm more in charge now of those areas of the play that puzzled and confounded me previously.

It's an emotional and physical kind of role. The man is clearly off his rocker, and very emotional from time to time, and bringing those two aspects into focus is not an easy task. Then again, because of my familiarity with the role, a lot of it is now beginning to ooze back. So one has a sense of repetition. James and Richard haven't done it before, which makes it more complicated. On the other hand I find

I'm wanting to go up alleyways I haven't been up before, and that is quite perplexing. I felt previously I had finished, and now suddenly other possibilities start to pop up. It makes it perhaps fresher, but it takes you away from the security of the part.

I have an image that Pozzo and Lucky were perhaps part of a law firm, that Lucky was one of the star pupils, and Pozzo got very attached to him. Then something went wrong, although deciding what it was is not so easy. I got this idea from Lucky's speech. I don't know whether Pozzo was completely taken by Lucky's charms, or whether they ever shared a life together. It's difficult to fathom and place into a realistic scenario. It comes back to playing the text: that's your principal guide, otherwise you go off the beam.

Friday 15 July

The afternoon is spent on exploring Vladimir and Estragon's relationship, trying to identify the beginning and end of each sequence in their emotional journey. Peter wants to pin down the changing balance in power between the two, who are so desperately dependent on each other, as well as the rapid shift in their emotions, and the thoughts behind them – for example, their alarm when they suddenly realise they may be in the wrong place.

As ever, he's concerned with the rhythm of the piece; it's almost as if he's conducting a musical score. 'It's not a pause there, it's a gapette,' he says at one moment, and at another: 'I can't quite explain why, but I think it needs a pause before that line.' He's also not averse to correcting the emphasis within a line, an approach which alarms and annoys many actors, but which James and Alan apparently take in their stride.

His concern with sub-text is much in evidence: he feels, for instance, that it's missing from the routine with the carrot and the turnip. Alan and James try it again, and immediately give it more depth. Peter also touches on one of the much-asked questions about the play: 'Is Godot an invention of Vladimir? Who knows?'

As the actors leave for the weekend, he talks to me further about the play.

Vladimir and Estragon have been together for many many years, they quarrel with each other, but they also help each other to exist. I don't know what they've done, they seem to be in a Franco-Irish country, and not England. But I think the only back story you can use is what you find in the text; imagining anything else can be dangerous for the actors, because it can limit them. It is of course a fiendishly difficult play to learn, because of all the repetition. That's why I asked them to learn it beforehand. But its musicality does help. My first response to it was certainly musical rather than philosophical; I responded to the cadences of the language.

It's a very poetic play, because of the precision of Beckett's words and his rhythms, and the way he uses all the old rhetorical crafts, like alliteration and antithesis and assonance. It's very much like the public utterance of the Irish Jesuit priest, especially in the case of Vladimir. And there's a tune to the piece which, if you get it right, is almost the same whoever acts it – though of course it's also a little different each time. These four actors are just about starting to fly, to be at a stage when you can direct them, where the language is almost instinctive and they don't have to think what they're saying.

Vladimir and Estragon are extraordinarily sophisticated people. But Sam wasn't opposed to the idea in my original production of them being tramps, although he never described them as such in the text. He once said to me, 'Do you realise they have gone round the world as tramps because of you?' I was actually quite appalled, I hadn't thought of that.

6 The Early Years

'Beckett has written about human distress, not human despair' – Actor Jack MacGowran

The successful 1955 London production of *Waiting for Godot* was almost immediately followed by other productions. In Europe the play again stirred up controversy, notably in Holland and Spain. In Holland it was attacked by the Catholic press, and threatened with a ban in Arnhem, on the bizarre grounds that it was a homosexual play. The threat only receded when the director and company threatened to resign *en masse*. In Madrid the church was again influential, and a ban was put on any advance publicity for a production in the university. As in Paris and London, there were often interruptions from the audience. During a production in Brussels, a woman stood up in the stalls and shouted furiously: 'Why don't they work?', to which a wit in the gallery replied: 'Because they haven't time.'

In Ireland the first production was put on in October 1955 at the Pike Theatre Club in Dublin. A converted coach house on the south side of the Liffey, it was away from the main city theatres in the centre, but in an area full of literary haunts. The building had been designed by the director Alan Simpson and his wife Carolyn Swift, former members of Anew McMaster's touring company. The tiny acting space was just twelve-foot square, and the small auditorium contained just 55 seats. In Beckett's view it was an ideal setting for the play, and in 1953 he had granted Simpson the rights to mount it there, and sent him his own English translation. However, because of the various problems arising in connection with the London production, and Beckett's desire for the first English-language version to be staged there, it was a further two years before the Pike production could open.

Dermot Kelly and Austin Byrne played Vladimir and Estragon, and Nigel Fitzgerald and Donal Donnelly were Pozzo and Lucky. Simpson's idea was that Vladimir and Estragon should be played as two down-at-heel Dublin characters who talked endlessly. He dressed them in torn, baggy suits and bowler hats, reflecting the music-hall element of the text. Pozzo was dressed as an Anglo-Irish squire complete with a military moustache, while Lucky was decked out in a ragged footman's outfit. In aiming in his translation to create a colloquial equivalent of his French original, Beckett had introduced various Irishisms, such as 'blathering' and 'your man', and Simpson added others, such as 'a bit of a gas' and 'bandjacksed'. (He also, to Beckett's annoyance, changed the opening line, from 'Nothing to be done' to 'It's no good'.) The Irishness of the production was reinforced by the colouring of the set, with the simple backcloth and sides painted in green, black and brown suggesting an Irish bog, and by the accents of three of the characters.

The advance publicity focused on the (British) Lord Chamberlain's objections to Beckett's alleged 'crudities' in the play, and the fact that the production had retained the passages which had been cut from the London production at the Criterion. The Pike management exploited this fact, warning people who planned to come to the play that, 'Many will find its philosophy and parts of its dialogue repellent.' In fact Dublin theatregoers remained generally unoffended, and the theatre was soon full most nights, sometimes to overflowing. After four months the production reached its hundredth performance, making it the longest continuous run in the history of Irish theatre. It then transferred across the river to the Gate, before touring a string of towns around the country.

The play had a mixed reception from the critics. Some, conscious of how the play had been received in London two months before, were wary about explaining its meaning. The critic of the *Irish Independent* dutifully wrote: 'The questions are posed, and there is no answer but the one which each member of the audience chooses.' In similar fashion the *Irish Times* reviewer, who compared Beckett to Aristophanes, argued that the plot was irrelevant: 'The interest is primarily in the comment, and the comment itself need not be consistent, full, or even always relevant.' However, some berated the play for its 'negative qualities' and its 'philosophy of despair'. Liam O'Flaherty dismissed it as 'tripe', while the reviewer of the *Evening Herald* judged that 'some of the grosser crudities...add nothing to the atmosphere, and are merely an attempt to out-Joyce the Joyce of *Ulysses*'. The reviewer in the *Dublin Evening Herald* felt the Dublin voices made it less moving than Hall's London production: 'Its tramps do not make the same impact, nor arouse the same pity. They merely look and sound like two chatty wayfarers.'

Despite these criticisms, Donal Donnelly's Lucky, 'a shivering symbol of servitude', made a great impact. As the production reached its hundredth performance in February 1956, Vivian Mercier wittily described it in the *Irish Times* as 'a play in which nothing happens, twice', a label which has clung to it ever since. He also suggested that the play appealed to the Irish audience because it laughed at despair. 'There is no object so sacred or intimate that an Irishman will not turn it to ridicule,' he wrote. The play may also have succeeded because, as the writer Fintan O'Toole later suggested, the clowning in the play bore 'an uncanny relationship to the kind of jokes that people in Ireland were making about the rather bleak nature of the place in the 1950s, when isolation and emptiness had a literal resonance in the depopulation of the countryside'.

All this attention and debate made *Waiting for Godot* a commercial success, and it quickly entered the popular culture in Ireland, becoming the subject-matter for cartoonists and pantomime artists alike. The title became a catchphrase, and an immediate response from anyone who was asked what they were waiting for. But three years later Beckett clashed with the Irish authorities. He had submitted some short works for the city's annual festival of plays and music, but when he heard that works by Joyce and O'Casey would not be performed because the archbishop of Dublin objected to them, he withdrew his own contributions. Enraged by the Catholic Church's bigotry, and the city council's fear of it, and remembering an earlier ban on his own books, he refused to give any further permission for his plays to be performed in the republic. It was to be a year before he yielded to pressure to lift the ban.

Meanwhile Donald Albery, who had the rights to produce the play in America, hoped that Hall would direct it there. One of the reasons Beckett had come to London was to give Hall and Albery his reactions to the Arts production. He suggested that, if they staged the Broadway version in his way, 'they would empty the theatre'. In the end Hall was not free to do it, and the American licence was passed to the producer Michael Myerberg. Beckett turned down several potential directors for the production. One was Sam Wanamaker, another was Leo Kertz, who had the intriguing notion of casting Buster Keaton as Vladimir and Marlon Brando as Estragon, a pairing which made Beckett's mouth water. His eventual choice, recommended by Thornton Wilder, was the young director Alan Schneider.

Myerberg was a producer admired for his risk-taking and innovation, but a series of bad decisions meant the play got off to a disastrous start in America. His first error was to open the production in Florida, rather than in places such as Philadelphia, Washington and Boston, where plays heading for Broadway were normally tried out. His second was to agree that the production should open the new Coconut Grove Playhouse in Miami, an 800-seat theatre with a Broadway-size stage, and a fountain in the foyer containing live goldfish. His third mistake was to advertise the play as 'the laugh of two continents', in a ill-judged bid to attract the local tourists.

His casting of the two principal roles was also misguided. As Vladimir he had chosen the light comedian Tom Ewell, and as Estragon the rubber-faced vaudeville star Bert Lahr, famous for his broad and grotesque performances in revues and musical comedies. Though both were stage actors, they were also film stars, famous respectively for *The Seven Year Itch* and *The Wizard of Oz*, in which Lahr played the Cowardly Lion. Their comic film stardom was highlighted in large type in the publicity for the show, while Beckett's name appeared in very small print.

Not surprisingly, the mink-clad, Cadillac-owning audience who came to the first night in January 1956 expected to see two famous actors in a farce. According to a local critic, the audience were 'more in the mood for *Guys and Dolls*', and when confronted instead with Tramps and Turnips, a third of them left during the first act. Another third failed to return for the second act, during which one woman allegedly announced as she stalked out: 'I paid for two acts, and this Beckett fellow only gives me one!' At the end there were three mild curtain calls, with Tennessee Williams and William Saroyan standing and shouting 'Bravo!' The press were hostile, the commentator Walter Winchell declared the work indecent and immoral, and Bert Lahr received a letter from an outraged member of the audience berating him for appearing in a play that was 'communistic, atheistic and existential'.

Rehearsals had proved painful. Schneider, who had seen both the Paris and London productions, was to become a fine interpreter of Beckett's work, and direct five further productions of *Waiting for Godot*. But at the time he was relatively inexperienced, and struggled to handle his errant company, in particular Bert Lahr. While Schneider wanted to achieve a balance between the comic and tragic elements, and to emphasise the play's ambiguity and subtle rhythms, Lahr was more interested in his own reputation, and in highlighting – and if necessary changing – the play's comic vaudeville routines. Asked to say what the play meant, he replied: 'Damned if I know!'

In his memoirs Schneider reveals some of the difficulties he faced. Although *Waiting for Godot* clearly demands an ensemble approach, Lahr was from the start apparently determined to be what he called 'top banana', arguing that

Ewell, as 'second banana', should act as his straight man and feed him the laughs. He tried to persuade Schneider to cut Lucky's speech, on the grounds that no one understood it, and that anyway they had come to see him, and not Charles Weidman. When Schneider resisted this notion, Lahr insisted on going off stage while the speech was delivered. As the opening approached, he continued to ad-lib lines and sounds which he said had worked for him in previous shows. Meanwhile Jack Smart as Pozzo, who had never managed to coordinate his stage business with his lines, refused to be directed, while Weidman, a trained dancer who had never before had a speaking part, found it increasingly hard to deliver Lucky's big speech – so much so that that on the first night he was unable to go on, and his understudy had to play the part. As for Ewell, he was, according to Myerberg, 'hysterical and impossible to control'.

Although business picked up slightly, after two weeks Myerberg decided to cut his losses and cancel the show, including the planned tour and the New York opening. A few weeks later he decided to re-stage it, with a mainly new cast, a simpler and more appropriate set, and Herbert Berghof replacing Schneider as director. Bert Lahr remained as Estragon, E G Marshall was the new Vladimir, while Kurt Kasznar and Alvin Epstein played Pozzo and Lucky. This time the publicity had a very different tone: Myerberg appealed for 'seven thousand intellectuals' to support the play, and suggested that 'those who come to the theatre for casual entertainment do not buy a ticket to this attraction'.

To many, *Waiting for Godot* seemed like a classic off-Broadway play, and with Beckett's backing efforts were made to persuade Myerberg to stage it in the Théâtre-de-Lys, where Brecht's *The Threepenny Opera* had recently enjoyed success. But Myerberg insisted on using a proper Broadway venue, the John Golden Theatre. Berghof knew the play well, having already directed an actors' studio production, in which he had played Estragon. In rehearsals he succeeded in gaining Lahr's confidence by allowing him to focus on the comedy, while Marshall (who had been to see the London production) provided more intellectual foil to his clowning than Ewell had done. Meanwhile Epstein worked privately on Lucky's speech, trying to determine its meaning, as he later recalled: 'I broke it down and tried to understand each bit, and what part each bit might have played in the whole when it was whole. It's like a smashed stained-glass window, a broken statue, and you have to find out where the pieces belong.'

This time the audience generally remained in their seats, and even stayed for post-performance discussions about the meaning of the play. Some critics were abusive, others baffled, a few appreciative. Eric Bentley was one of the latter, noting that 'highbrow writers have been enthusiastic about clowns and vaudeville for decades, but this impresses me as the first time that anything has successfully been done about the matter'. Tynan suggested the play was 'transfigured' by Lahr's performance (which it clearly was). 'Mr Lahr's beleaguered simpleton, a draughts player lost in a universe of chess, is one of the noblest performances I have ever seen,' he wrote. Brooks Atkinson of the *New York Times* was intrigued: '*Waiting for Godot* is all feeling,' he wrote. 'Perhaps that is why it is puzzling and convincing at the same time.' Norman Mailer apologised for a previous attack on the play, which ran for ten weeks and over a hundred performances, and established Beckett's name in America.

The second US production came about on the other side of the country, and in very different circumstances. The avant-garde San Francisco Actors' Workshop had been founded in 1952 by Herbert Blau and Jules Irving, who taught at the city's state college. Since then they had been putting on productions of European plays then little known in America, including works by Brecht, Genet, Ionesco and Dürrenmatt. In 1957 Blau, who had seen a lot of theatre during his travels in Europe, decided they should mount a production of *Waiting for Godot*.

Blau later reflected on the changing attitudes to Beckett's work: 'I think the hardest thing to reconstruct, now that Beckett has been deified among American theatre people, particularly academics, is just how startling those plays were.' Among the first to be startled were members of his company. After the first readthrough in Blau's house in Haight-Ashbury two of the older, more experienced actors dropped out. Blau recalled: 'They had always been suspicious of my experimental tendencies...but with *Godot* they thought I was crazier than usual. When they read through the play they simply didn't know what was going on, which didn't seem to be much, and much of that they didn't like.' Replacements were found, but then before the first night the actor playing Vladimir left. His replacement, a Catholic, was reportedly dubious about the play's apparent despairing philosophy, but stayed with the production.

For the actors the rehearsals were a difficult time, and a lot of talking took place. The play seemed to them to subvert all the normal conventions of plot and character, crisis and resolution. Trained, if at all, to approach a role via the psychological interior method of Stanislavsky, they now had to work in a different way. Blau persuaded them to think of themselves as performers, stripped of any conventional ideas about character, and not to concern themselves with psychological realism or Beckett's meaning. 'Just perform what he tells you to perform, and you will feel, as if by some equation between doing and feeling, exactly what you need to feel, and in the bones.'

Such was the scepticism about the play within the company, it was decided not to present it as a full-scale production, but initially to offer it to the theatre's subscribers as an 'alternative' show, to be played only on Thursdays. But gradually the production began to gain attention, the audiences grew, and the number of performances was increased. Soon the play became a cult phenomenon, and before long it was moved into the main repertoire, where it remained for several years.

This production was obviously closer in spirit to Beckett's intention than the version staged on Broadway, being much bleaker and less benign. It also had one unexpected and bizarre outcome. Initially panel discussions were set up to follow the Thursday performances, featuring not just the actors and director, but also a psychiatrist, an academic and other professionals, who would all answer questions. Soon several men in the audience started to stand up and say how much they identified with Lucky, who had been played as an androgynous figure with many feminine qualities. This was the Fifties, a time when gay men were not supposed to admit to their supposedly deviant sexuality. The panel discussions were abandoned.

Thereafter the play was frequently performed, although in New York it was usually in off-Broadway theatres. It also became popular in universities and colleges, and in the more adventurous regional theatres. Among other directors, Alan Schneider soon returned to it, directing a production at the Alley Theatre, Houston, while Herbert Blau staged it at the Encore in San Fransisco.

It was not long before film and television offers were made for *Waiting for Godot*. In principle Beckett was resolutely opposed to the idea, believing his plays were unsuitable for screen treatment. In 1959 he turned down an offer of $25,000 from Paramount Pictures and Bert Lahr. But sometimes he wavered in his attitude. Shortly afterwards a proposal for Peter O'Toole and (possibly) Peter Sellers to star in a film version looked a strong possibility, but stalled at the contract stage, and Beckett eventually vetoed the idea. Later Dustin Hoffman expressed a desire to play Estragon, and Hall was approached to direct it, and asked if he would persuade Beckett to sell the film rights. He tried, but the plan never got off the ground.

Beckett reluctantly gave his consent to a television production, broadcast by the BBC in 1961, with Jack MacGowran and Peter Woodthorpe as Vladimir and Estragon. In order to preserve the unity of the play the director, Donald McWhinnie, used a single camera. Beckett, visiting London, watched it with McWhinnie, the actors, and his publisher John Calder, and was clearly unhappy with what he saw: 'My play wasn't written for this box,' Calder remembered him saying afterwards. 'My play was written for small men locked in a big space. Here you're all too big for the place.' With radio, however, he was more comfortable. Although the BBC had initially failed to secure an agreement in 1955 to broadcast *Waiting for Godot*, Beckett soon after became very keen to write for radio. The result was *All That Fall*, directed by the newly converted McWhinnie for what was then the Third Programme.

After the Arts production others, both professional and amateur, were staged in Britain. One of the first, directed by Denis Carey at the Bristol Old Vic in 1957, featured the young Peter O'Toole as Vladimir and Peter Jeffrey as Estragon. In 1961 the play found a different audience at the Theatre Royal in London's Stratford East, a working-class area and the base for Joan Littlewood's revolutionary Theatre Workshop. Directed by Alan Simpson, it featured Brian Phelan and David Kelly in the principal roles. The play also entered the amateur repertoire, where it often aroused indignation. David Girling, then a schoolboy, remembers how a 1956 production at the Guildford Theatre Club baffled and irritated many around him in the audience. 'There was a lot of chatting, a lot of people getting very fidgety, and sometimes saying quite loudly, "What on earth's all this rubbish about?"' Sometimes the response was more drastic: when a company came to perform the play in Scotland at the Abbey theatre in Arbroath, the entire audience walked out.

Productions of the play gradually spread beyond Europe and America. By 1968 it had been played in more than twenty different countries, from Finland to Argentina, and translated into fifteen languages, including Serbo-Croat and Japanese. It was already becoming a topic of interest among academics, who subjected it to all kinds of theoretical, philosophical and aesthetic analyses, offering a variety of meanings and interpretations. Some undertook a close

7 Rehearsals: Week 3

Tuesday 19 July

The focus at the start of the day is on the final pages of Act 1, after Pozzo and Lucky's exit. Immediately they've gone there's a characteristic exchange between the other two:

> VLADIMIR: That passed the time.
> ESTRAGON: It would have passed anyway.
> VLADIMIR: Yes, but not so rapidly.

Beckett has a pause before the next line, but Peter takes the unusual step of over-riding the author, suggesting they drop the pause. 'The rhythm here is exquisite,' he says. Focusing on the text, he frequently conducts it gently with his right hand as the actors speak their lines, then asks for 'a hair's beat' here, a 'tiny silence' there. His comments are often couched in the language of music. 'You need to rest on the rhythm a bit more,' he suggests at one moment. 'You're picking up on each other's intonations too much. This is really a duet, so allow the other person their space.'

This section includes the short scene with the young representative of Mr Godot. Two boys have been cast to alternate in the part, but both live in Bath, and won't be joining rehearsals until the company moves down there. Meanwhile Alan and James have the slightly weird experience of addressing their lines to an empty space, while Cordelia reads the Boy's part from out front.

Peter encourages them to bring out the increasing despair in their situation, and the darker emotions. 'Be angrier,' he tells James. 'It's a little panic attack.' James: 'It's about charting the depression, deciding how vulnerable he is.' Alan: 'You're rising above it, and I'm sinking below it.' They work on it in further detail, then run through the whole scene. Peter: 'Good. This is very fine, and not a false note than I can hear.'

During the lunch break designer Kevin Rigdon talks to me about the set.

Peter generally gives you a very wide design brief, a general idea of what he wants without asking for specifics. I think the difficulty with this play is creating a world that is at the same time specific and not specific. You're not looking to create a naturalistic space. In Bath we're having to work within the limitations of a repertory season, where the exits and entrances are a given, as is the stage floor I designed, which has to work for all the plays. For *Godot* you've basically got a confined space, in which the actors can only go in one direction or the other.

I felt strongly that the rock had to be a real rock. A papier mâché or plastic one would look false. Then there was the tree: is it dead? is it weeping? We did some research and came up with a first idea. Peter's comment was, It's a very interesting tree, but it's your tree, not Beckett's tree. So I re-designed it, sketched it out, and pared it down to a simpler version, with almost a scarecrow and human shape. The aim was to achieve a balance on the stage between the location and size of tree. As for the leaves, we had to decide what kind they should be, new growth or old growth? We spent an afternoon in Kew Gardens, and looked at a variety of leaves before coming up with a pleasing shape. I think the notion of mature growth works better because of the connotations of life springing forward.

The moon was quite a challenge. We originally looked at the idea of one piece sliding open to reveal it, but that became very elongated, so we decided we could split it. Once we came down to what we thought was the right size of the moon, that dictated the size of the panel and the rest of the panels on the set. Peter felt the idea of a blue surround was appropriate. Then I felt that it would be useful to have a horizon line, just a very subtle one, to give another angle to it.

During lunch Peter has been reading some of the reviews of his original production. 'Let's do Act 2 of what Bernard

Levin called our "twaddle",' he announces as the rehearsal resumes. Once again he draws the actors' attention to the sudden swings that occur in their emotions, and where the shifts come. 'One minute Vladimir is full of compassion, the next moment it's, I don't want to know about your fucking dreams.' James and Alan practise the hat-changing routine, which has become a little solemn. 'We need the sense of kids playing a game,' Peter observes.

The frequent repetition of certain phrases still occasionally causes the actors to lose their bearings. In the middle of the carrot and radish scene Alan is pulled up by Donna for giving James the wrong cue.

> ALAN: I thought that was in the second half.
> JAMES: This is the second half.

James is now completely off the book, which immediately improves the flow of the work. The two actors' styles of movement are noticeably different: Alan, a natural clown, is precise and economical, James, the more extrovert character, is more open and free-flowing. They complement each other wonderfully well. 'Terribly good,' Peter tells them at the end of the day.

Wednesday 20 July

Today the work starts at Pozzo and Lucky's entrance in Act 2. Terence now has a pair of knee pads to cushion his fall; Richard has a vivid red and yellow harness to prevent any damage to his neck. Their fall as they come in, with all the clutter they are carrying, needs several attempts before it develops a reasonable shape. The same applies when first James and then Alan are added to the complicated heap on the ground: it's proving hard to make it look real, and a good deal of time is spent on it.

Peter is still picking up on tiny details, giving tiny textual corrections and emphases, suggesting the emotional changes. 'It's a bit of a pause there – make it a silence,' he tells Alan. 'More anger there, it's the married couple again,' he says to James. Later he says, 'It's because of Estragon's pretentiousness that Vladmir replies so sarcastically.' When they reach the line 'All humanity is us', he suggests they adopt the pose of Rodin's 'The Thinker'. They do so in music-hall fashion, to good comic effect.

In the afternoon they switch back to the start of the play. 'This opening section is quite abrasive,' Peter says. He wants James to be slightly bitchier at one point, Estragon more sarcastic at another. Overall he's clearly looking for a harsher tone, while retaining the comedy and the warmth of the Vladimir/Estragon relationship. Eventually they run the first section of the act. 'Terrific, it's really alive,' Peter comments. 'It's working very well.'

Mark Lawson from the radio programme *Front Row* has come in to watch the last hour. His smiles and chuckles suggest he has been enjoying it. Afterwards he takes Peter off to do an interview for the programme. I stay on to listen to Trish Rigdon talk about designing the costumes.

This is one of the most difficult jobs I've ever done, and a bit terrifying at first. Peter's brief was, Don't make a statement. He made no reference to tramps or clowns. These are just broken-down people, they're in garments they've been in for a very long time, and these are the only garments they own. We talked about bowler hats, but he felt they were too specific.

The difference between the two characters is emerging in the lines of the costumes: Vladimir, the more masculine and vertical character, has a coat with straight lines and straight pockets, and a straight hat, whereas Estragon, a more rounded and feminine character, has a jacket which is shorter and curved, and his hat is round. Pozzo is a land-owner, with a connection to the land and the earth, so we chose browns and greens, and a rich-looking plaid, and his waistcoat is made out of cashmere.

Many of the clothes, though they look like rags, are having to be custom made. For Estragon we are having a frock-coat made, and then we will break it down. His trousers have to be 52 inches to drop to the floor, so they have to be made, and we need to sew in weights so they will be sure to fall. And for Lucky we need to find a hat which can fit three characters.

Friday 22 July

A film unit from the *South Bank Show* are in to film rehearsals – they're showing a two-part programme in October and November on Peter's life and work, to mark his seventy-fifth birthday. With two cameras, microphones, wires and half a dozen people squeezed into what space there is left in this small room, it's beginning to resemble the overcrowded cabin scene in the Marx Brothers film *A Night at the Opera*.

This morning it's Pozzo and Lucky's central scene. Terence's Pozzo is increasingly powerful, and his ode to the sky is bleak and poignant. Along the way he queries a couple of Beckett's stage directions. Peter responds: 'After you say Pan sleeps, there's a very long silence, in which the play should die. The audience should wonder if anything is going to happen. And in the long silence before you start Lucky up, I think you're reluctant to set off any of it, because all of it is awful. Even the dance is grotesque.'

At one point there's a light-hearted exchange about Beckett's supposedly sacrosanct text:

TERENCE: Can we change the order of the lines?
PETER: Ooooh!
TERENCE: To something in a previous version.
PETER: Ah. (*He and Cordelia consult the Beckett Bible.*) We'll buy that.
TERENCE: Good.
PETER: But don't get any ideas.

Richard's walk is now more grotesque, and in the Think he is getting more variety in the pace, and finding different levels to look out front. Peter gives him some brief notes. 'The greater range in your voice helps a lot. The separate layers and levels are very good. Give more emphasis to

Fartov and Belcher. Make waste and pine more lyrical. Slow up on Fulham, Peckham – we're on the brink of Fuckham.'

They run the whole section, which is now beginning to come together. At the end of the day I pick up a few comments from the actors.

> JAMES: I need to find a lightness of touch. At the moment I feel like I'm hitting it all with a heavy hammer.
>
> ALAN: You have to get the rhythm right, but I think James and I are interacting well with each other. Like most double acts Vladimir and Estragon are different types. We don't have a great contrast, so I'm busy bending at the knees to try to look smaller.
>
> TERENCE: There's a terrible temptation in the first act to make Pozzo real, when he's somebody who is rather mad. If you start applying rational thoughts to the text, you go astray I think.
>
> RICHARD: The thing about the long speech is being able to concentrate while everything is going on around you. As I don't speak anywhere else, I'm recalling the speech in my head at every available opportunity – even when we're doing a run-through of a section.

8 Prisons and Politics

'Man, that was my life' – Prisoner in San Quentin jail,
after a performance of Waiting for Godot

The universality of Beckett's play is underlined by the
many contrasting environments it has been played in over
the last half century, and the many different audiences
it has spoken to. Its impact has been especially remarkable on those thousands of prisoners of many nationalities who have seen a production. It has also, like many of
Shakespeare's plays, provoked many different resonances
around the world, depending on a country's cultural or
political circumstances.

Founded in 1952, the San Francisco Actors' Workshop
had played to many different audiences in California during
its short existence. But the one to which they presented
Waiting for Godot in November 1957 was quite different
from any they had known previously. It consisted of four-
teen hundred inmates in the San Quentin prison, watched
closely by armed guards strategically positioned around the
vast dining hall in which the performance took place. No
theatrical event had been seen at California's oldest prison
since Sarah Bernhardt had presented a Shakespeare anthol-
ogy there in 1913.

The invitation to stage the play had come from the
prison authorities. The company first thought of bringing
Arthur Miller's *The Crucible*, but then discovered no females
were allowed inside the prison. When they opted instead
for *Waiting for Godot* there was initially some resistance.
According to the director, Herbert Blau, the prison psychiatrist was put off by the supposedly depressing nature of
the play. He also felt it would be too obscure, and even
traumatic, for the inmates. He couldn't have been more
wrong. The performance, played on a makeshift stage at
one end of the dining hall, provoked a sensationally positive

response. Nothing could have underlined more dramatically the capacity of the play to have meaning for people living in all kinds of circumstances.

Anticipating a rough ride, Blau addressed the audience first, warning them not to expect a conventional play or a straightforward story. Minutes before, the prison band had been playing some jazz, and this gave him his cue. 'This play has a theme like a piece of jazz,' he explained, 'and there will be riffs off the theme, and then you will come back to the theme.' He compared the play to a piece of jazz music 'to which one must listen for whatever one may find in it', and hoped that each member of the audience would draw some personal significance from it.

The prisoners were held. The prison newspaper the *San Quentin News* announced that 'the San Francisco company had its audience of captives in its collective hand'. A play which had initially baffled critics and intellectuals in America and Europe seemed crystal clear in its meaning to a group of men facing an empty future. Several of the inmates wrote articles in the prison paper showing how it related to their own situation. Rick Cluchey, a lifer, described how he and many others reacted to the startling arrival of Pozzo and Lucky. 'Suddenly there was no confusion about the warden's role and my own convict dog boy's ass. I too had a lifetime rope round my neck. Everybody in the audience reacted. Waiting, the play was about Waiting!' Many prisoners had clear views about the play's meaning, as they told a local reporter present at the performance. 'Godot is society,' said one. Another said: 'He's the outside.' A teacher at the prison observed shrewdly: 'They know what is meant by waiting…and they know if Godot finally came, he would only be a disappointment.' The *San Quentin News* also demonstrated the level of identification the prisoners felt with Beckett's characters: 'We're still waiting for Godot, and shall continue to wait. When the scenery gets too drab and the action too slow, we'll call each other names and swear to part for ever – but then, there's no place to go!'

The performance had such an impact on the prison that, in Blau's words, the language of the play and the names of the characters became 'part of the therapeutic vocabulary at San Quentin'. It also led the prisoners to seek permission to start their own drama group. Permission was eventually granted in 1961, partly in the hope that it might reduce violence within the prison. According to Cluchey certain conditions were attached: there were to be no female impersonations, and 'no plays which held a dark mirror up to the law, society or the establishment'. Interestingly, Beckett's plays seemed to cause no difficulties in this respect. In the next nine years the San Quentin Drama Workshop staged 35 productions, including seven of Beckett's works. The first was *Waiting for Godot*, followed by *Endgame* and *Krapp's Last Tape*. Cluchey, who was later pardoned and became a friend of Beckett, was inspired by the San Francisco Actors' Workshop production to write his own play, *The Cage*. The former gallows room at San Quentin was turned into a 65-seat theatre, and Alan Mandell, an established actor and member of the Workshop, came regularly to the prison to provide classes for the prisoners in acting, directing and stagecraft. Later in 1970 a group of prisoners was parolled so they could tour a production around America.

Beckett's play was subsequently staged in other American prisons, again with unexpected results. A performance in the Florida State Prison was marked by a great deal of audience participation. According to one of those involved, Sidney Homan, the action was constantly interrupted by prisoners shouting out questions. At first this frustrated the actors, but soon they began to reply: 'Here was an audience, these men waiting, who demanded to be part of the production, who took what we said so seriously that they could not remain silent,' Homan recalled. 'By the second act the audience was collaborating with us, both in performing and in thinking about the performance.'

As a result of this remarkable development, the play lasted three hours instead of the normal two. At the end the warden ordered the men to line up to return to their cells. Instead, to the horror of the actors, they broke ranks and started running towards the stage. It turned out they just wanted to talk about the play, and about how they identified Godot with some aspect of their prison lives. This they did, with each actor and crew member coordinating a huge group of the men. 'The discussion was informed and eloquent beyond anything I had ever known in the class-room,' Homan remembered.

A further testimony to the power of the play to speak to those waiting for freedom came from Jan Jönson, who left the Royal Dramatic Theatre in Stockholm to direct it in the Swedish maximum security prison of Kumla. 'A prison is the right place to stage *Waiting for Godot*,' Beckett had told him. The inmates came from many countries, including China, Spain, Honduras, Portugal and Russia. 'It was very hard work for them, because it really opened them up,' Jönson said. 'Strange, heavy, very heavy reactions. And they cried. One of the inmates said, "Do you know what is happening here? You are giving me my life. This play is my diary. What Vladimir is thinking and talking about is me." For him the play was a kind of primal scream.' When Beckett saw the video of the production, he told Jönson: 'I saw the roots of my play.' The production went on a national tour, which came to a sudden and unexpected end just before the first night in Gothenburg, when four of the five actors, all drug offenders, escaped through a dressing-room window.

Jönson was subsequently invited to direct the play in San Quentin prison, thirty years after the San Francisco Actors' Workshop had made their first visit there. This time the cast of prisoners played to some three hundred people, includ-ing actors and directors from Europe and America, seated on wooden benches in the gymnasium. As before, the actors had no problem in linking the play to their situation. 'Prison life is like the play,' said Twin James, who played Vladimir. 'Part of that text was part of me, crying out. In it was all the agony and pain that I felt. I am no actor, but in order to play that character I didn't have to act.'

Since its early days *Waiting for Godot* has achieved a startling political impact in many countries, especially those where there is oppression or inter-racial conflict, or where people are waiting patiently for change. Because it is a metaphorical rather than a naturalistic play, and because it is full of ambiguity, audiences can more easily relate it to their own lives or the society they live in. As Martin Esslin has written: 'When *Waiting for Godot* was performed in Poland, everybody there knew who Godot was – the freedom from the Russians, which can never come. When the play was done in Algeria during French rule there, the audience of landless peasants immediately knew that the play was about the promised land reform that never came.'

The play's performance, and sometimes just its publication, has often been banned by the authorities, though not always for the same reasons. One of the first productions to run into trouble was the one staged at the Belgrade Drama Theatre, only a year after the original Paris production. Like a lot of works from the West, *Waiting for Godot* was considered 'decadent' by the powerful writers' union of the Communist Party. The theatre was so nervous about staging the play they decided to exclude the audience from the first performance and, after a protest by intellectuals, to ban all further performances. A second performance took place privately before an invited audience in an artist's studio, but it was another two years, by which time the political situation had improved slightly, before the play was put on professionally. Staged at Atelier 212 in Belgrade, it was the first production to be seen in any of the Eastern European communist countries. It was soon followed by the first one in Poland, staged in Warsaw in 1957.

At this time cultural repression was also strong under fascism in Franco's Spain. Most works were banned, especially those from abroad. Such experimental theatre groups as existed managed to perform works by Camus, Sartre, O'Neill, Miller, Claudel and Ionesco, but they could only get licensed to put on a single performance in very small theatres. *Esperando a Godot* was actually refused a licence in

1955, on the grounds that it was 'obscure and obscene'. As a protest against this stifling of artistic freedom, it was staged in the university in Madrid. This was as much a political act as an artistic statement, provoking the playwright Fernando Arrabal to comment: 'If this is the kind of drama being performed in Paris, I shall go there.' Two productions the following year in Madrid and Barcelona caused a considerable stir. As in London and elsewhere, the play divided its audiences and provoked extreme reactions: Beckett was labelled a fraud and a snob by some, a genius by others.

In South Africa *Waiting for Godot* and Beckett's other plays were not performed for many years. Along with other writers deeply opposed to the repressive apartheid regime, Beckett refused to allow his plays to be performed in any theatre which practised racial segregation. But in 1976 he gave the go-ahead to a *Godot* production planned by the new Market Theatre in Johannesburg, with a multi-racial cast, a black director, and a guarantee that there would be no racial discrimination in the sale of tickets. It was a time of deep unrest in the country, with demonstrations and riots leading to further political repression. The director and actors – in the end it was an all-black company – took great risks in travelling to rehearsals, and the volatile situation also affected audience numbers. But the play was well received by the local critics, and although the number of black people in the audience gradually grew, the authorities left the theatre alone.

Soon afterwards the black actors John Kani and Winston Ntshona were arrested for performing Athol Fugard's *Sizwe Bansi is Dead*, a savage critique of the apartheid regime. It was the same two actors who, four years later, played Vladimir and Estragon in a mixed-race production sanctioned by Beckett. Directed by Donald Howarth, it was performed at the Baxter Theatre in the University of Cape Town, and also played in America at the Long Wharf Theatre in New Haven, Connecticut, and in London at the Old Vic. 'With a multi-racial South African cast, the play assumes different tonalities,' the critic Mel Gussow wrote. '*Godot* is a play of infinite resources, and each version I have seen accents specific motifs.' Although the set did not suggest any particular locality, Howarth's casting of two white actors as Pozzo and Lucky, and his dressing of Pozzo to look like a Boer farmer, gave the production a strong local resonance. While it was not an overtly political production, with Vladimir and Estragon bonding playfully, Pozzo's master–slave relationship with Lucky became in itself a powerful statement about the apartheid regime.

In China the play was considered dangerous, and was not even allowed to be published, although it was known about in intellectual and theatrical circles. Any work linked to it was likely to face trouble. In 1983 Gao Xingjian, who later won the Nobel Prize for Literature, wrote *The Bus-Stop*, a play directly inspired by Beckett's banned work. It concerned a group of people from the suburbs who wait for a bus to take them into the city: the bus never comes, and they realise they have wasted their time. *Waiting for Godot* was recognised as the inspiration for the piece, which was denounced by the authorities as 'the most pernicious play put on since the birth of the People's Republic'.

Few productions can have been more overtly political than the one put on in 1984 by the young Israeli director Ilan Ronen in the Haifa Municipal Theatre. It was staged at a time when relations between Israel and Palestine were in a particularly poor state. Previous Israeli productions of *Waiting for Godot* had stressed the stylised elements. 'We placed the tramps in the here and now,' Ronen explained, 'in the belief that this would add another dimension to the play's boundless potential.' Vladimir and Estragon, played by Arab Israeli actors, became Palestinian labourers working on a building site in Israel, with Pozzo and Lucky, played by Jewish actors, as their Israeli foreman and his Arab slave. The translation was a bilingual one, a mixture of Hebrew and Arabic: Vladimir and Estragon spoke a vernacular Arabic with each other, but Hebrew to Pozzo, while Lucky used literary Arabic. The production proved controversial, and several members of the Knesset, the Israeli parliament, demanded the production be banned, arguing that it was being used as a propaganda tool for the Palestine Liberation Front. Ronen's response emphasised how the non-specific setting of *Waiting for Godot* allowed for many different kinds of production: 'Without our having changed one word of Beckett, the play lent itself beautifully to the political treatment, as if it were intrinsic to it.'

The production in 1991 by Joël Jouanneau at the Théâtre des Amandiers in Nanterre was also of a political nature, but aimed specifically at a young, working-class audience living in a dreary suburb of Paris, many of whom faced a life of unemployment. Jouanneau set the play in an urban wasteland, with Vladimir and Estragon as drifters in woolly hats. An unusual feature was the big difference in their ages: Estragon was played as a young, aggressive skinhead in his twenties. Substantial cuts were made to the text, and the actors improvised some sections so it could be updated into the street language of the time. While the production was praised for its beauty, it was also felt the play had lost its crucial element of anguished comedy.

It took a long time for many of the East European countries to allow the play to be performed. The first production in East Germany was not until 1987, while in Bulgaria it took place the following year, and was seen as a contribution to the struggle for artistic freedom. One of the more remarkable productions was staged in Yugoslavia in 1993, during the siege of Sarajevo by Serbian forces. The director, the American writer and director Susan Sontag, declared: 'Beckett's play, written over forty years ago, seems written for and about Sarajevo.' Sontag made use of local theatre professionals, whose livelihoods had been interrupted by the siege. Without electricity, rehearsals had to be held by candlelight, as did the performances, which were confined to matinees because of the dangers of people going out at night. For a terrified population, living under constant bombardment and uncertain what the next day would bring, the play's themes of uncertainty and emptiness clearly echoed their own desperate situation.

Partly to involve as many of them as possible, but also to underline the general representative nature of the characters, Sontag used three Vladmir/Estragon pairs: one male couple, one female, and one mixed. It was not the first time that women had appeared in a production, nor would it be the last. Beckett was fiercely opposed to such experiments, arguing that he wrote the characters as men, and to have them played by women changed fundamentally the nature of the play. 'Women don't have prostates,' he remarked once, referring to Vladimir's bladder problem. But to his annoyance several productions, including one staged in Israel in 1973, went ahead without his permission. Some of the reasons given to justify using women bordered on the bizarre. In Japan one director defended his decision to have a female Vladimir and Estragon by stating that women were more used to waiting than men.

Over the years Beckett turned down numerous requests for permission to stage the play with actresses. One that he rejected vehemently came from the Hollywood pair Shelley Winters and Estelle Parsons, who wanted to mount a production with themselves in the starring roles. During the 1980s several women's theatre groups performed the play without permission, or without making it clear to Beckett or his agent that the actors were to be female. In 1991 an amateur company called Taboo staged an all-female production in Galway. 'We weren't interested in making a statement, we just wanted to do it,' its director Nora Connolly says. 'We didn't make any concessions to the cast being women. There was no discussion about Vladimir and Estragon's talk about hanging giving you an erection. The important thing was the words, and the play's philosophical poetry.' The group was invited to bring the production to the Focus in Dublin, but were then threatened with an injunction by the Beckett estate, which called their action 'an abhorrence'. In Dublin the show was attended by Barry McGovern and other actors who had appeared in past productions in Ireland. 'They were very supportive,' Nora Connolly remembers. 'They said that if we were banned, they would come along and play it for us – in frocks.'

The most serious and public dispute arose in 1988, when a Dutch company, de Haarlemse Toneelschuur, continued with their all-female production against Beckett's wishes. They too played the text as Beckett wrote it, and played the characters as men – although they set the play in a palace, with Vladimir and Estragon expensively and fashionably dressed. This time the dispute went to court, with Beckett's lawyer arguing that the integrity of his text had been violated. The judge read the play, saw the production, and found against Beckett, on the grounds that the performance remained close to the dialogue and followed the stage directions. He ruled that 'since the play was about the human condition in general, it transcended the sexual identity of men and women'.

Beckett's attitude to the notion of an all-black production of the play was more ambivalent. 'That's my best news,' he remarked in September 1956, after hearing of one such production. With Rex Ingram, a well-known film star, playing Pozzo, and Earle Hyman as Lucky, it opened successfully in Boston, but ran for only five performances on Broadway, an artistic success but a commercial disaster. Later, however, Beckett felt that the unusual casting was a distraction for the audience, preventing them from concentrating fully on the play.

What these and the many other productions demonstrate is that, whatever Beckett's reservations about certain kinds of productions, *Waiting for Godot* is susceptible to being performed in almost any environment, allowing audiences to extract their own meanings from a play that seems to remain forever modern.

9 Rehearsals: Week 4

Wednesday 27 July

This morning the actors attempt a run-through for the first time. I notice that in the two days I've been away several changes have occurred:

- There's much more tension and atmosphere.
- There's been a general tightening of the action.
- Everyone is virtually word perfect, so cues are picked up more precisely.
- There are several move changes.
- A real carrot has appeared, and Alan munches it happily.
- Terence's voice is even more menacingly resonant.

Lucky's speech has also developed significantly since last week:

- Richard has discovered how to foam at the mouth.
- In his dance he now seems at the end of his tether (as, literally, he is).
- There's a change in the timbre of his voice: he sounds older.
- He's found more variety, which makes the content easier to grasp.
- As the speech reaches its climax, the others have become increasingly distressed.

In the interval, while the actors take a coffee break, Peter gives me his thoughts about the progress of the production.

It's at a very interesting stage. The shape and form of the play is so calculated by Beckett that you need a tremendous discipline to learn what he's actually written – which doesn't only mean the words, but the pauses and the silences and the hesitations and all the rest of it. The actors are just beginning to make it their own, just beginning to make you think that they're inventing what they're saying rather than repeating it. Of course it's a tricky play to do, it's like learning an intricate dance step or fight.

Alan has been here before, and is keeping his courage up, but I think James is getting abreast of him now. Terence is an amazement to me, I don't quite know where it's coming from, he's getting wilder and more anarchic, and funnier than he was when he did it before. He's drawing on something from his own psyche, which is quite alarming. Richard is magnificent, he's absolutely wonderful. His speech makes more sense now in a completely insane way. He's taking it slower, which I think is probably an advantage.

I think it's in a very healthy state; they've just got to practise it. I may be wrong about this, but I think giving them masses of notes at this particular stage will actually increase the formality of it, rather than give them the freedom that they need. Over the next couple of weeks I will go through it with them line by line – but not until they've notched up their freedom, which they haven't quite done yet. Once they've achieved that, I'll start imprisoning them, and they'll have to break out again – it's a series of oscillations. It all comes down to whether you start from form or from instinctive improvisation and freedom. I obviously think you should start from form, particularly with this play.

This time round I think I'm more aware of Sam's central obsession, which is death, why, how, what is it, what happens. I suppose it's because I'm older, but I'm very much haunted by the mortality of it, that gets more powerful. On the other hand the play seems to be slightly less abrasive this time. I don't know why yet, and I don't know whether it should be. I shall probably roughen it up a bit.

The actors return, and run through Act 2. Again I notice several developments:

- James' Vladimir has become more vulnerable at key moments.

- Alan's Estragon is angrier than before.
- The routines are more explicitly rooted in the music-hall.
- It's now truly rapid fire in the cross-talk.
- The falling into a heap is improved, but still not believable.

Afterwards Peter gives the actors his notes.

The Pozzo and Lucky scenes are working very well: they're completely understandable and wildly funny. Lucky's speech is enormously powerful, and more disturbing – it's coherent and clearer. Vladimir and Estragon have a terrific emotional relationship. It could open on Monday, and be perfectly credible.

You've honoured the text, it's a perfectly learned intricate dance. But you need to get free in the form, it's not quite cohesive. The words are there, the steps are there, you just need to practise it until you can do it in your sleep, and make it yours. And then you need to tell me and Cordelia what you need beyond that. We must work through it line by line to find the kind of *Godot* we are doing. Perhaps we need to make it more abrasive and harsh? I feel it needs to be bleaker.

It's a great, great play. The rhythm of the writing is so potent. Sam would say, If you get it the way I wrote it, you can get like you want it to be. What you're doing is very fine. It would do now, but we want to take it further.

Thursday 28 July

Peter starts the day by looking in detail at the parts he felt didn't work yesterday. One of these is the hat-swapping routine:

PETER: This worries me. I can't read your emotions, why you are doing it. Is it competitive, and if so, when? Or is it a duet?

ALAN: He's trying the hat on, and I'm imitating him.

JAMES: Yes, and I have to assume Estragon is my mirror.

> PETER: So you need to copy each other precisely, and sepa-
> rate the actions each time.
> JAMES: On the last hat, we have to get over the point that
> neither of us wants it.

After several attempts, the routine begins to make more sense – and is more amusing as a result.

Peter asks James to make more of Vladimir noticing the tree has suddenly gained leaves. 'That moment should be beautiful. But his reference to things having changed needs thinking about. It's terribly ambiguous: it shows that there is time and so there is hope, but there is also death.' He also observes of their discussion about the leaves: 'In this duet Vladimir and Estragon at first achieve satisfaction and peace, but then there's silence, which points up the anguish of saying nothing at all.'

They next run the difficult section where Pozzo cries out for help, and is initially ignored, and finally all four characters end in a heap on the ground. Suddenly a mobile rings. 'It's Godot again,' Alan says. In fact it's his own phone, which he finds and switches off. Vladimir continues: 'I begin to weary of this motif.' And the phone rings again... Despite these interruptions, the scene is coalescing better. 'It's a wonderful section,' Peter says. 'It's people chattering away while something dreadful is happening. If we can play it at full cruelty, it will top the first act.'

Over lunch I ask Terence and Richard how they think they're progressing.

> TERENCE: Peter seems to approve of what I'm doing with
> Pozzo. He's a difficult character to play, but I do seem to
> have an instinctive feel for the role, though I'm not sure
> why. But I still need to work on the quality of his blind-
> ness in the second act, and what his motivation is in the
> scene.
> RICHARD: We have to make the text sing, and I think we're
> beginning to do that. Peter has thoughts, but he doesn't
> impose them, which is good, because I think every actor
> has to find their own truth and their own physical world,

as long as it doesn't impose on other people's perform-ances. Very little has changed in my head about Lucky's journey and history. I think he was once a beautiful thing, incredibly intelligent, but Pozzo has enslaved him and destroyed him, and beaten all the humanity out of him. It's an incredibly demanding role, emotionally and physically and mentally and spiritually, firstly because he doesn't speak, and secondly when he is spoken to he's treated like dirt – Hog! Pig! If I let that get to me it would be terrifying, but I don't.

After lunch, as they work on the same section, Peter tries to point up more sharply the contrast between Vladimir and Estragon. 'Estragon is depressed, whereas Vladimir is excited that Pozzo and Lucky have come,' he suggests. 'Vladimir is the suit, the leader, the politician. It's a side of him we haven't seen before, fighting for his identity, being very mean and just wanting to save number one. Estragon can be more easily diverted, he's more reactive, like an animal.'

As always, he's willing to consider and explore ideas offered by the actors. One of these comes when Vladimir and Estragon are looking out into the wings from opposite sides of the stage: Alan wonders if they might introduce an echo at the end of their calls to each other. They try this out, and it seems to be effective, though Peter warns: 'I'll get people saying the only discernible difference between this and your last production is the yodelling.'

Friday 29 July

The day starts with another attempt to get the timing right of Pozzo and Lucky's complicated entrance and exit. It's still quite disorderly and unconvincing, and is clearly provoking a certain amount of frustration. This comes to the surface when Cordelia asks the actors which of two alternatives moves would suit them best.

TERENCE: Don't ask us, tell us.

PETER: I'll remind you of that.
TERENCE: I'm sure you will.

It's a rare moment of tension, and it passes immediately.

James and Alan test out their synchronised walking, which is now impressively precise. 'Very good, very delicate,' Peter comments. But he's less happy about another bit of business he suggested previously. 'I don't like the Rodin "Thinker" pose. Let's just try it with hands on heart: the shit of patriotism.'

They reach the moment when Pozzo reveals he is blind. Here, Peter suggests, there needs to be an abrupt change in Vladimir and Estragon's attitude: 'This section should be informed by kindness and compassion for Pozzo. You're going through a tremendous purgatorial experience, and now with his blindness it's become a simple human situation. Once you've helped Pozzo up, the tone is one of all passion spent. There's a certain Biblical rhythm: I always think Vladimir went to a Jesuit college.'

James and Alan quickly find the right note, without it becoming sentimental.

At the end of the day I ask them how they feel the work is shaping up.

JAMES: There's an instinct to make a line more comfortable for yourself by making it colloquial, which is often what you have to do on scripts. But when you have a great play structured as well as this one is, you've got to play its game. That's where Peter has been so helpful, with his great skill on the text. When you take over a part there's usually a sense that you've got to hurry up because the others are waiting for you. That's never happened here with Alan, who's a colossal help. His skill as a clown is fantastic, and I've found that very valuable.

ALAN: I have to be careful not to stick to the rhythms of the previous production while working with James. It's slightly different this time, but not enormously so, because the rhythm is very clear and precise. The problem we're facing at the moment is to try to fit all our physical action into that rhythm, rather than let it break it up. So we need to run it, in order that we can hear the whole concerto, rather than just the separate movements. It seems to be written in sketches, which all have to fit together, with each one having a different tone to make the whole piece. But we're getting there.

10 Beckett the Director

'I know no more about this play than anyone who just reads it attentively' – Beckett

Between 1966 and 1984 Beckett directed productions of his major plays in London, Paris and Berlin, using scripts and making notes in English, French and German. When he wrote *Waiting for Godot* he had no knowledge of the playwright's craft or any detailed experience of the theatre. He wrote it, he admitted later, without imagining how it would work on stage. Yet from the start he was extremely interested in how directors aimed to stage the play, and liked to be involved in rehearsals. Before very long he started directing himself.

His method was very different from that of other directors. As early as 1953, during the first Paris production of *Waiting for Godot*, he refused to explain the play's meaning or the background of the characters. As he later put it to Alan Schneider: 'If people want to have headaches among the overtones, let them. And provide their own aspirin.' This attitude caused conflict with many actors, who were used to understanding their parts intellectually, and bringing to them their own interpretations. Jean Martin, who played Lucky in the original production, complained: 'Becket does not want his actors to act. He wants them to do only what he tells them. When they try to act, he becomes very angry.' But Lucien Raimbourg, who played Vladimir, had a different view: 'I've never in my life met someone so profoundly human, so modest and yet so clear in explaining what he could see or not see in the characters through the acting.'

By the time the play was revived at the Odéon in Paris in 1961, Beckett had meticulously noted all the movements that he wanted, and intervened much more in rehearsals, evidently with Blin's approval. Deirdre Bair, Beckett's first biographer, described the scene in the theatre: 'He became a definite presence at every rehearsal, a brooding force of which the directors and actors were always aware, smoking endless cigarettes, hunched into a third-row aisle seat or peering over the shoulders of the technicians backstage. He demonstrated movements to the actors, told them how to sit, to walk, to fall. As usual he ignored their probing, puzzled questions, and directed their attention to their exterior movement and speech.'

In 1964 *Waiting for Godot* had its first London revival at the Royal Court, this time, to Beckett's quiet satisfaction, in an unexpurgated version. George Devine, the Court's artistic director, had a good professional and personal relationship with Beckett – he had directed *Endgame* and *Happy Days* at the theatre – and invited him to come over from Paris to assist with the production during the last two weeks of rehearsals. The director was Anthony Page, who had cast Nicol Williamson as Vladimir, Alfred Lynch as Estragon, Paul Curran as Pozzo, and Jack MacGowran, one of Beckett's favourite actors, as Lucky.

'When he arrived we ran the play for him, and then we talked,' Page recalls. 'He had seen many productions by then, and had a very clear idea of how it should be done. He was particularly clear about the tones of voice to be used, and also the movement. He was completely authoritative, and it all worked. We didn't have any arguments; for me it was a relief to have him there. But he disliked theorising, and didn't want to discuss the play's meaning.' Beckett did ask for one change, suggesting the warm, muddy-brown set be re-painted grey, to help convey better the feelings and ideas within the play.

'It was a very easy and happy experience,' Page says. 'The actors loved working with him, and so did I. He seemed to enjoy the process, and the play grew very well with him there.' Beckett thought Curran outstanding, and told his friend John Calder that Williamson had 'a touch of genius'. But he and the company had to endure a moment of crisis when Williamson suddenly disappeared from rehearsals, and couldn't be found for a few days. Page finally tracked him down in someone else's house, lying on a bed with his face to the wall. 'He was having a kind of mini-breakdown, and took a lot of coaxing back again. Beckett had to wait in the theatre, but he was very patient and concentrated, and didn't create a stink as he might have done.'

The production was a success, but as always, hating to watch the play with an audience, Beckett stayed away from the first night. Such occasions were agony for him, as the playwright David Storey discovered a few years later. During the first night of one of Beckett's own productions, Storey came across him in the bar of the hotel near the Royal Court. 'When I inquired why he wasn't watching, he replied: "I can't stand the pain." I said: "What of?" "The mistakes," he replied, and went on to explain that every performance was inevitably different, by however faint a degree, from how he had envisaged and directed it.' One of the elements that mattered most to him was the precision of the text's rhythm, as was made very clear one day while he was directing *Happy Days* at the Court, when he brought a metronome into rehearsals, placed it on the floor, and said: 'This is the rhythm I want.'

The following year he was once again involved with *Waiting for Godot*, but in very different circumstances. He had a call from the Schiller Theatre in what was then West Berlin, asking him to rescue a production of *Warten auf Godot* being directed by his friend the dancer Deryk Mendel. Rehearsals were well advanced, but the actors were struggling to learn their lines, and there was animosity between them and Mendel, who in their view was putting too much emphasis on the metaphysical meaning of the play. Beckett's presence calmed matters somewhat: he concentrated as usual on concrete questions. It was though a grim experience for him: one actor, whom he found undirectable, gave what he described as the worst perform-ance as Pozzo he had ever seen. To his surprise, however, a production that he considered mediocre was liked by both critics and audiences.

Ten years later Beckett returned to the same theatre, this time to direct the play by himself, using his German translation. By now he had substantial experience of directing his own work, including productions of *Endgame*, *Krapp's Last Tape* and *Happy Days* that he had worked on in the Schiller's studio theatre. This new staging of *Waiting for Godot*, which opened in March 1975, was to be seen as a landmark production, reflecting most clearly Beckett's intentions and his view of the play.

He approached his task in an unusual manner. For months he had been thinking about the play, and had made detailed notes about re-shaping it, including meticulous descriptions of the moves, complete with arrows and diagrams. He told his assistant, Walter Asmus, that the play was a mess, that he hadn't visualised it well enough when he wrote it, and that he now wanted to 'give confusion a shape through visual repetition of themes; not only themes in the dialogue, but also visual themes of the body'. With this in mind, he made hundreds of cuts and revisions to both the text and the stage directions, which were later incorporated into the English version.

In rehearsals he worked to give more emphasis to repetition and contrast – of words and themes, gestures and movements. His role often seemed as much that of a conductor as a director, as he would often beat out the rhythm of the text with his hand. He concentrated also on the visual elements, aiming to create precise patterns in the movement of the characters. He used the word 'balletic' to indicate the precision he was looking for. Asmus explained his motive in doing so: 'It was not that he wanted them to move like ballet dancers. It was simply to express that there was a design in the blocking that had meaning. Movements step by step on a line or a word, or a crossing in silence, had to do, for example, with the reunification or separation of Estragon and Vladimir, who belong inseparably together. The design of the movement structure tells the story of the relationship of the characters to one another.'

Although the actors got on well with Beckett, and did their best to please him, there was an underlying tension in rehearsals, resulting in part from his refusal to discuss meaning. If the actors questioned him about the realistic connotations of the play, he would respond with comments such as 'It's all poetic', or 'It's a game, everything is a game'. Yet despite his rigidity and evasiveness, he was still open to suggestions from Asmus or the actors, and many of the visual gags were worked out on the spot rather than pre-planned. But his perfectionism, and the gap between his vision of the play and the actors' ability to realise it, led inevitably to disappointment. 'You could see when Beckett believed in what the actors were doing, and when he didn't,' Asmus recalls. During rehearsals Beckett wrote to friends telling them he was fed up with hearing the words, felt unfitted to direct actors, and was sick of the theatre in general, and *Waiting for Godot* in particular.

The production, however, was a great success. 'It was an evening of surprises and of extreme intellectual pleasure,' the critic of the *German Tribune* wrote. 'The comedy was constant, despite its desperate nature.' Yet the same critic pointed out that Beckett had not dispelled the mystery that surrounded the play: 'He has not broken his silence. He merely puts on the stage what he has already recorded in his script. His four wonderfully human protagonists give a truly sensational performance, but none of the puzzles are solved.' In fact the production divided opinion amongst Beckett's friends and theatrical associates: while some thought it wonderful and beautifully orchestrated, and very funny, others felt it lacked vitality, with the actors resembling automatons. Asmus remembers it being 'very beautiful and stylish, and precisely choreographed'.

The production came to the Royal Court the following year, as part of a season of plays to mark Beckett's seventieth birthday. Peter Hall saw it in both countries. 'It's the best production I've seen, its precision was extraordinary. It held in balance absolutely perfectly the pain and the agony and the abrasiveness with the comedy and the absurdity. To be hyper-critical, it was slightly too meticulous, there was a feeling of constraint about it. But in London it was much looser: the actors were doing the same things, but much more freely.' The critic Michael Billington suggested that it exploded the notion that writers should not direct their own play. 'Beckett's production of this stoic masterpiece is devoid of either easy pathos or forced fun,' he wrote in the *Guardian*. 'This spare, exact, marvellously clean production shows that *Godot* is infinitely more than either slapstick tragedy or awesome cultural monument.'

In 1984 Beckett became involved, as a favour to his friend Rick Cluchey, in a production by the San Quentin Drama Workshop, to be staged at the Adelaide Festival. He was very reluctant to be drawn in, and only agreed to 'oversee' the production if it was directed by Asmus, who had staged the play in New York six years before. The company rehearsed for several weeks in Chicago, after which they met up with Beckett in the Riverside Studios in London. Mentally and physically tired, and at seventy-eight less meticulous and obsessive than of old, Beckett still spent ten days moving the production in the way he felt it should go. He was even moderately satisfied with the result, declaring that 'the production, generally speaking, is now very presentable'.

Though not everyone shared Beckett's belief that he was the best interpreter of his own plays, his work as a direc-tor had a strong influence on others, whether they initially worked with him, like Asmus and Schneider, or merely came to see his productions. Yet as he did with actors, Beckett blocked all attempts by directors to get him to shed light on the play and its characters. When Schneider asked him, 'What does it mean?', he replied, 'It means what it says.' Later he observed: 'I couldn't give the answers which were hoped for. There are no easy solutions.'

11 Rehearsals: Week 5

Tuesday 2 August

The actors arrive to find three large mirrors covering the wall at stage left. They've been brought in so that Alan and James can polish their routines, and get absolutely in step.

> PETER: Do you like yourselves?
> ALAN: I'd forgotten I look like that.
> JAMES: I've fallen in love with Estragon all over again.

Before they begin to rehearse properly, Peter suggests they need to make certain parts of the play bleaker. 'The human and comedic content of what you're doing is very sound, so we can afford to hurt the audience. The play has not yet become as big as it should be in the moments of greatest despair. It's a mosaic of differing emotions, and the transitions are difficult.'

They then run the first ten pages uninterrupted. Parts are smooth, parts are rough. 'I'm moving too much,' James says. Alan observes: 'I feel the pauses are a little long around the tree.' Peter continues to make small adjustments. 'I know Sam says you both have your arms dangling here during the silence,' he tells them, 'but what you did belongs to another convention, it didn't contain the emotion, it seemed empty and contrived.' Alan suggests a different, less symmetrical stance, which overcomes the problem. They run the section again. 'Good,' Peter says, 'you treated each other like a couple who have been together for years, so it's no holds barred.'

During the break there's a brief discussion about the Bath season, which as well as *You Never Can Tell* includes *Much Ado about Nothing* and *Private Lives*. Coward's play is about a crazy couple tied inexorably to each other – like Vladimir and Estragon. Should he perhaps have staged them in tandem, Peter wonders?

After lunch Alan and James run Act 2, excluding the Pozzo and Lucky section in the middle. Peter is delighted: 'It's terribly good, the emotional size is much larger,' he says. 'The power stops it seeming to be the same as Act 1, which of course it isn't.' But there are still points where he wants more harshness, and as they run it again he points them out: 'The anger's a bit late in coming… There should be more guilt there… You need more anguish, it's a very dark moment… Make it more conspiratorial… It should be more desperate, more fragmented.'

He's still concerned to highlight the difference between the two characters. 'Estragon's function is not to change,' he suggests, 'but Vladimir goes on a terrible journey.' As usual the actors chip in with observations.

ALAN: Estragon is becoming more and more desperate.
JAMES: Vladimir is finding it harder to calm him down.
ALAN: What annoys him is that he can't remember anything.
JAMES: His despair comes like sudden holes in the text.

On the whole their discussions are to do with individual lines and moments, not with more general meanings.

At the end of the day Peter remarks: 'Every time I come back to this play, it seems more of a masterpiece. It's wondrous. But why, when it's pessimistic, does it send people out feeling good?'

Wednesday 3 August

Terence and Richard join again, this time for a canter through Act 2. Terence is now decked out in a check jacket and waistcoat, which gives him even more of an upper-class air than before. At times he is terrifying, like a roaring buffalo; at others poignant and touching, especially now that he is bringing out his blindness more clearly and intensely.

There are still tricky technical hurdles to overcome. Pozzo and Lucky's entrance and exit still lack coordination and precision, and the fall into a big heap is still clumsy and unconvincing. Understandably, everyone is being a bit careful not to hurt anyone. But the tension in trying to get the physical side right makes them lose their rhythm, and occasionally forget their lines. Peter suggests that when Vladimir and Estragon join the pile they might stylise it a little, and this seems to help.

Later there's a brief exchange about the leaves on the tree – should they be three instead of five, to reflect Christ and the two thieves on the cross? Peter checks in the Beckett *Notebooks* before concluding: 'There are a lot of academic theories, but Beckett says they're just there to show the passing of time.' Later he checks what the Beckett Bible has to say about another line, but then loses patience with it – 'Oh stop it!' – and closes it firmly.

Over lunch Richard talks to me further about the Think, and what he sees as its possible meaning.

> I think the speech is developing well. The more I look at it, the more I realise what's in there. The through-line is becoming much clearer to me. Basically I think it's this: that given that man perceives there is a God, given that we are capable of immense things and great thoughts and incredible works of art and literature, ultimately we waste everything that we have, and we pine the loss of everything that we gain. So it all boils down to the fact that, no matter how much we strive, it's all in vain. That's incredibly bleak. The references to tennis and hockey and football – these civilised things are a very brittle veneer over humanity, they're just frills. Ultimately, underneath everything, there is nothing. That's what Vladimir is analysing the whole time. He's saying, There must be something. But ultimately there isn't, you just get what you see. Man is not this incredible spiritual being. There is no God ultimately, and if there is, we will never understand him. It all comes down to the fact that we eat and drink and piss and shit, and we look to the sky and try to see things that probably aren't there.

After lunch the actors move on to the end of Act 2, and the second appearance of the Boy. James is still having to address an empty space, with Donna now reading the Boy's lines. Despite this handicap, his despair at the realisation that Godot is again not coming is very moving. 'It's a real journey into blackness, Vladimir can't bear it, it's the same boy again,' Peter tells him. 'But your indignation allows you to find those extraordinary images without being sentimental, and that's excellent.'

Later they go back to certain moments that require refining or re-examining. Peter clearly feels that James and Alan have found most of the nuances in their characters' complex relationship. Alan has developed enormous power in his most desperate moments, while James is skilfully charting the many subtle shifts in Vladimir's emotions. 'You're getting far more emotional anguish, which gives the play a larger dimension, but also highlights Vladimir's stoicism,' Peter tells Alan. 'And there's an inner desperation about you both, so the whole thing feels more crisis-ridden.'

As they break for the day Peter concludes: 'It's become terribly good.' James replies, with feeling: 'It's a fucking hard play.' Peter: 'It is, but if we get it right, it's limpid and simple like no tomorrow.'

Friday 5 August

This morning there's a run-through, mainly for the benefit of Peter and the actors, but also so that members of the production team can see the whole play for the first time. The small audience that squeezes into the cramped room include Trish Rigdon, the sound designer Gregory Clarke, Jerry Gunn the company stage manager, the voice coach Majella Hurley, and Danny Moar, the Bath producer.

The next two hours are a revelation. Suddenly the play has taken off. It has become funnier and at the same time more alarming. It's no longer a technical exercise, but an afternoon of palpable emotion, the contrasting elements of the piece blending together as they never have done before.

The words seem new minted. All the hard, detailed work of the last five weeks – on rhythm, timing, meaning – is now paying off. The presence of an audience, however small, has put steel into the actors. James and Alan have made Vladimir and Estragon's desperate need for each other more vivid, their friendship more touching. Terence seems to have found, apparently from nowhere, new dimensions to his interpretation of Pozzo, making him both madder and sadder. Richard yet again has given more variety and edge to the Think; the moment when he takes off his hat to reveal his grey hair is quite shattering.

When they finish Peter, clearly moved, gives his verdict.

Well done. I'm not exaggerating when I say that's the best account of the play I've ever seen, here this afternoon in this strange little room. So I'm rather tearful.

A few notes. First of all, the tragic dimension of Pozzo is there in a way I've never seen before. Second, the absolute horror of what Lucky is trapped in is there in a most disturbing way: it was absolutely terrifying, and magnificent. And the contrast between Vladimir and Estragon is both less and more. The physical life is working remarkably well: it's not gagging, it looks as if they have always been together. What's also interesting is that you've appropriated aspects of each other. That's because you're playing together so beautifully. And the idea that Vladimir has problems which in isolation he works out, and Estragon is sitting on his stone quite happily day by day – that's gone. It's now purgatory for both of them, for both of you, and I thought that was terrific.

The first act is terribly clear about the persecution of Lucky by Pozzo. The second act is really upsetting: the callousness of Vladimir and Estragon towards Pozzo, which you've never had before at the right level, is now there. James the intellectual, slightly professorial person, is really wonderful, and Alan's Estragon has now become a truly tragic figure. Your performance, Terry, is truly alarming – and that's meant to be the highest praise. It's very upsetting, and I think the burghers of Bath will be running for the exit doors.

I've always felt, with the balance between the comic and the tragic in the play, that one earns the other: if it's rightly comic it's horribly tragic, and if it's horribly tragic it needs to be comic. But it's bloody hard to get that balance, and you truly hit it this afternoon. It really is magnificent, and I can't thank you enough. It's in wonderful shape, and we've got to be very careful to keep it that way. When it's put into a theatre space, with people watching and laughing at it, it will take on another dimension. So we've got an exciting time ahead of us now, bringing it to the boil.

And so to Bath.

12 The Later Years

'Godot will always be viewed as Beckett's Hamlet *or
his* Ulysses' *– Actor Barry McGovern*

Once Beckett lifted the ban on his plays being performed
in Ireland, *Waiting for Godot* was staged there many times,
most notably at the Abbey and the Gate theatres in Dublin.
The Abbey mounted its first production in 1969. Directed
by Sean Cotter, it had Peter O'Toole as Vladimir and Donal
McCann as Estragon. Beckett, who disliked O'Toole, was
furious when he heard about the production: owing to a
mix-up, the licence had been granted by his agent without
consulting him. He did his best to stop it, but it was already
in rehearsal, and all he was able to do was to get the run
limited to a month.

The play had a mixed reception from the audience: 'I
loved it, but others didn't,' the actor Barry McGovern recalls.
One critic wrote approvingly of O'Toole's Vladimir 'bubbling
and soft-shoe shuffling in indefatigable Micawberish optimism between the abysses of despair…protecting the
incurable carping pessimism of Donal McCann's Estragon in
beautifully balanced and timed counterpoint'. The *Sunday
Independent* announced that history was being made, that
with this production the Abbey had now truly become
Ireland's national theatre.

Des Cave, who played Lucky, remembers the impact
it made. 'It shook the place up a bit. Sean was a very
meticulous director, and he made it an iconic production.
The set, with its grey windswept sky, was reminiscent of
Connemara, and O'Toole and McCann, with their tuxedos
and bowler hats that had seen better days, looked like a
pair of dishevelled city gents.' Like most actors he found
Lucky's big speech very difficult to learn. 'But once I had it
in my head, I found it fascinating. It was the only part I've
played where I had to go to the gym to get fit in order to

stand still.' He needed to keep his concentration during the speech, as O'Toole and McCann pretended to play rugby while he was delivering it.

The play's continuing power to shock the ordinary theatregoer was shown the same year, when an amateur drama group started by the father of Jim and Peter Sheridan, both young Beckett enthusiasts, staged a production in Ireland. Peter Sheridan remembers the reaction: 'We took it around the amateur drama festivals, where we received a mainly hostile response. They were used to seeing John B Keane and the old Irish plays, they'd never seen anything like this, and they found it really obtuse. "This is not a play," people shouted out.' A decade later he directed the play at the Project in Dublin, Ireland's first arts centre, set up as a protest against censorship. 'Once done, you don't forget the play,' he says. 'It stays in the subconscious. I last directed it twenty years ago, and I can still remember almost every line.'

In 1982 Ben Barnes, who was to work on many Beckett plays, directed *Waiting for Godot* for the Irish Theatre Company. Later, while working on another production of it, he talked of his desire to remain faithful to Beckett's text and stage directions. 'The play is a trademark theatrical and physical Beckett challenge, with the actors confined on the stage the way we're confined by any city or country we live in. As a director I have never considered myself reverential towards the masters, but because I have complete faith in Beckett's theatre and his vision, I am content to follow his instructions to the letter.'

It was this company, playing in a touring production at the Project not long afterwards, that provided a unique moment in the stage history of *Waiting for Godot*. After Pozzo's entrance, Vladimir and Estragon discuss whether he might in fact be Godot, to which Pozzo replies: 'I am Pozzo! Does that name mean nothing to you?' One night the actor, Kevin Flood, declared: 'I am Godot! Does that name mean nothing to you?' It did of course, but it left the actors in a tricky position. Needless to say the surprise twist in the story brought the house down. It may have been this incident which inspired Alan Titley's play, staged in 1990 at the Peacock, the Abbey's studio theatre. It was called *Godot Turns Up*.

Undoubtedly the most celebrated production of the play in Ireland was the one directed by Walter Asmus at the Gate. First mounted for four weeks in 1988, it was revived there for the Beckett Festival in 1991, and returned several times in subsequent years. After assisting Beckett in Berlin at the Schiller, Asmus had directed a production himself at the Brooklyn Academy of Music (BAM) in New York, with Sam Waterston playing Vladimir, Austin Pendleton as Estragon, Michael Egan as Pozzo, and Milo O'Shea cast as Lucky. While based closely on Beckett's own Berlin production, it contained more comic interplay with the audience. In Dublin he again used Beckett's production as a model, aiming to retain its rhythm and dynamics. But he also made it clear that his version would not and could not be identical. 'I don't just re-create,' he said. 'The set and costumes are different. The actors are different. That means the overall atmosphere will be different. It's always a new creation, a new and exciting experience. You never really know where you are going. You put a different emphasis on different aspects of the play, or you discover entirely new aspects. Your own experience of life has increased, and that flows into the new production. In Dublin I tried to make the dialogue simpler, more low key.'

One element that changed after the first Dublin production was the set by Louis le Brocquy, one of Beckett's many artist friends. Originally it had flats on the side, with scribbles and colours on them, and a road going into the distance painted on the horizon. Later it became much simpler, with just black flats, a simple, grey hazy screen, and a tree. 'It worked much better,' Asmus remarked. 'The stage had been beautiful the first time, but too busy.' Another difference from Berlin was the speed of the production. 'In Dublin they have a very good command of language, and Irish people talk a lot,' Asmus observed. 'I expected the audience to a certain extent to know the play, so the problem was to find a pace, a very fast pace. We speeded it up tremendously, and that worked, because the two main actors worked together very well. The chemistry was just right.'

His chosen Estragon was Johnny Murphy, while Vladimir was played by one of the foremost Irish interpreters of Beckett, Barry McGovern, who in addition to appearing in the plays created *I'll Go On*, a one-man show based on Beckett's novels *Molloy*, *Malone Dies* and *The Unnamable*. 'Although *Godot* is not set in Ireland, to anyone who lives here it's redolent of the country,' he says. 'Its rhythms are Irish, it smacks of Irishness. At the same time there's something universal about the play. I love playing in it, although when you come back to it again and again, it's difficult to come up with something fresh. You don't want to do it differently just for the sake of it, but at the same time you don't want it to become a museum piece.'

The universality of the play was underlined when the Gate production toured to America and several other countries over the years, performing in cities as diverse as Seville, Chicago, London, Los Angeles, Toronto, New York, Beijing and Shanghai. In China the mere fact of the production being there emphasised the marked difference in attitude towards the play from that of twenty years before, when it had been banned. It was staged in 2004 before a mixed Chinese and foreign audience, with a simultaneous translation shown on side-screens, and was extremely well received. 'The audience was quiet at first, but then they gradually began to catch on to the humour,' Barry McGovern recalls. The *China Daily* critic described the play as 'complex, difficult and occasionally incomprehensible', but saw the production as 'a once in a lifetime experience... sheer theatrical magic'; and one that needed 'a dictionary of superlatives to praise it properly'. Asmus remembers that 'Lucky was the focus. The audience were stunned by this poor creature with a rope round his neck. I think it had political implications for them.'

The production also toured to Melbourne in Australia, where the play had first been staged in the late 1950s in the small Arrow theatre. In 1976 a particularly striking production with an overtly Australian setting was performed in a theatre in Monash University, directed by Peter Oyston. Vladimir and Estragon wandered aimlessly in the hostile setting of the Outback; Pozzo was portrayed as the colonial oppressor, and Lucky, an Australian aborigine, as the colonial slave. Later, Neil Armfield staged a notable production with the Company B Belvoir as part of the 2003 Sydney Festival, an event which also included a six-day symposium on Beckett, attended by a hundred scholars from around the world to mark the fiftieth anniversary of the first production of *Waiting for Godot*.

In America the play gradually became a staple part of the repertoire, playing in many universities and colleges as well as commercial theatres. Staging it was now clearly a much less risky venture commercially: in 1971 an Off-Broadway production starring Paul E Price and Henderson Forsythe ran for nine months. Audiences and critics around the country were more accepting, and less puzzled. 'Twenty years ago, when the play was new, everyone was trying to figure out what it meant, and it all had to be a symbol of something else,' Dan Sullivan wrote in 1977, having seen a performance in the Los Angeles Actors' Theatre, directed by Ralph Waite. 'Here the question of meaning never comes up. Like any good story, it means itself.' In 1981 Alan Schneider directed it again in the Public Theatre in New York, and during the 1990s there were many productions in regional theatres, in Chicago, Sacramento and Reno among other places.

Beckett called the play a 'tragi-comedy', and the best productions were generally those that achieved a careful balance between the two elements. But some took the comic element to extremes, the most notorious being Mike Nichols' production at the Lincoln Center in New York in 1988, labelled by one critic 'Godot with pratfalls'. Steve Martin played Vladimir and Robin Williams was Estragon, with F Murray Abraham as Pozzo and Bill Irwin as Lucky.

Beckett was clearly nervous about the production, as Walter Asmus recalls: 'He wanted me to ask Mike Nichols if I could sit behind him and tell him what to do. He was very naïve. Mike laughed when he heard, and said, Sure you can come – but then I was offered the Gate production.'

Nichols' basic idea was to make the two main characters homeless New Yorkers. In rehearsals Williams promised to play the role straight, with no comedian's additions, but once confronted with an audience he quickly broke that promise. 'Throughout the production Williams does a complete pantomime, with only slight reference to the text,' one critic wrote. This was particularly in evidence during Lucky's speech, when he borrowed a programme from a woman in the front row, giggled when he found his name in it, then shared the joke with Martin. As the speech continued he shouted at Irwin, 'You're a liberal!', a mocking reference to the recent presidential campaign. He and Martin pulled out the stops for the music-hall routines, but the play effectively became a farce, gaining plenty of laughs but losing its essential bleakness and the characters' basic dignity.

In the Far East that year a very different kind of clown was on show, in a production more likely to meet with Beckett's approval. Martin Esslin, then head of drama at the BBC, visited a Korean production in Seoul. It was a highly stylised one, with Vladmir and Estragon being played as 'real clowns, whose movements are so closely coordinated that they at times become almost balletic'. This style, reflecting the non-realistic approach of much of Eastern theatre, seemed to Esslin admirably suited to Beckett's play. He found the gags more gentle and stylised than in Western productions, 'making the play more like a symbolic statement, more philosophical, and more dreamlike'.

This non-naturalistic approach to the play was also in evidence in Japan, where links were made between Beckett's work and the formalised style of Noh theatre, the tradition in which many actors were trained. The first production in Japan had taken place in 1960, and others followed, usually done in a very stylised way. The play became very popular: in the period 1972–92 there were ten productions, as well as sixteen adaptations loosely based on the play. In Tokyo in 1994 Japan's best-known director, Yukio Ninagawa, staged one of the boldest experiments, using two companies, one male and one female, which played on alternate evenings. The women, wearing bowler hats, performed as if they were men, but wore tattered geisha kimonos. Ninagawa's aim, he said, was 'to reveal the classic status of Beckett's work, stripped of all theatricality'.

Roger Blin continued to work on the play, directing another production in Paris in 1978. It was a measure of the distance *Waiting for Godot* had travelled that, twenty-five years after its opening in a tiny Left Bank theatre, this production was performed in the heart of the French theatrical establishment, at the Comédie-Française. Blin spoke of the play's continuing appeal to a wide age-range: 'Spectators who saw the play twenty-five years ago were afraid that they wouldn't feel the same effect in seeing it again. But they told me that the actors recaptured the spirit. As for the younger generation who were afraid it would be old hat, they were struck by the work's modernity.'

A much-admired production was one directed by Luc Bondy, which opened in Lausanne in 1999, and toured widely in Europe. Bondy believed that Beckett's own production had stifled the actors' ability to find a sub-text for their characters' actions. His was an inventive production full of powerful images, but generally faithful to Beckett's text and stage directions. Other productions were less so, although few went as far as André Engel's production in Strasbourg in 1979. Staged in a disused hangar, and 'inspired by' *Waiting for Godot*, it mixed extracts from the French version of Beckett's play with other events, including a rape and a terrorist attack, in a setting which included a café and shops, and two parked cars.

A less radical re-interpretation was George Tabori's 1984 production in Munich, which began as a rehearsal of the play around a table, and only gradually metamorphosed into a full rendering of it. Beckett reportedly squirmed when he heard about this 'concept' production, but then, curiously, authorised a film version. In his later years he evidently became more relaxed about the play being transferred to another medium. Shortly before his death he allowed Asmus to make two video recordings, one of the French text and one of the revised English one.

By then the play was being performed all over the world, as it continues to be on the eve of the centenary of Beckett's birth. It has also reached a younger audience, having become a set text in schools, colleges and universities. In 2004 Asmus returned to the play, directing a production for young people in a small theatre in Ventura, California. 'I believe the play goes on being staged because it deals with everyday problems,' he says. 'We can transfer it to our own experience. Fifty years ago it led to all those discussions about God and Existentialism. Now twelve-year-olds come and see *Waiting for Godot*, understand it, and go round quoting it.'

13 The Final Rehearsals

Monday 15 August

A theatre. A stage. Early afternoon…

The actors have finally arrived at the Theatre Royal in Bath, ready to embark on the technical rehearsal. In the auditorium Peter and Cordelia are sitting towards the back of the raked stalls, behind a makeshift desk fitted over the seats in front of them, while Kevin, Trish and others are dotted around elsewhere. Behind the directors, in the front row of the low dress circle, sits Peter Mumford the lighting designer, and behind him Gregory Clarke the sound designer, each with their desk housing the appropriate computerised equipment. Donna too is there, in touch through her headphones with stage manager Jerry Gunn and his team, who are working behind the scenes.

While waiting for the actors to appear in their costumes, Peter waxes lyrical about the Bath theatre, where his company has been based for the last three years. 'I think this is my favourite theatre in the country. Next to the Haymarket, it's the best proscenium theatre. The sight lines are simply wonderful, these stalls and the proscenium arch make virtually a square, and overall it's a really beautiful classical theatre.' He's also very pleased with Kevin's set. 'I like its beautiful neutrality,' he says, looking out at it. 'It doesn't make any statements.'

The actors emerge on to the stage one by one, and start to gauge its size and sniff its atmosphere. Last week they worked in a rehearsal room in Bath, running the play several times, and generally, in Alan's words, 'getting a sense of the shape of the wood rather than the individual trees, doing a little titivating, touching it up, tying up loose ends, clarifying areas, so that the whole thrust of the piece is clear'.

Before the rehearsal starts the tree's position needs to be finalised, so the stage management, with James and Alan in attendance, try various options. Once Peter is satisfied they nail it into place. The actors then start to run Act 1. After all those weeks watching them close up in their everyday clothes, it's something of a shock to see them in the distance, fully costumed: suddenly they *are* their characters.

As they move through the act, they have to stop frequently and wait patiently as Peter Mumford experiments and discusses with Peter various lighting options. A thin hazy mist is tried at the beginning, but cut because it's too distracting. Sometimes the tree is too brightly lit, at other times the amount of light on Vladimir or Estragon needs adjusting, to lessen the contrast between their faces. Often the actors have to continue playing while a sequence of lighting cues from an earlier section is tested.

During a break Peter Mumford, who's worked often with Peter but never previously lit a Beckett play, tells me how he's approached this one.

Peter talked a little about Beckett's attitude towards light, which was basically, Give us some light, electrician! We discussed how things had changed and in some ways improved since those early days, giving you many more possibilities. However, you don't want to feel that there are big lighting changes every time something happens. There are fifty cues on the show, and if you looked at them individually you would see there are a lot of changes; but it shouldn't seem like that to the audience, they should blend and flow. So we've kept the lighting very simple. We're using a lot of moving lights, and I've kept to a palette that by and large uses only them, rather than any cross-fading lights. So the characters move the lights around the space, but in a very gentle way: it's like weather, like clouds passing. It's about clarity, with the actors becoming the scenery.

I think the blue background works very well, but we have to be very careful to make it both a room and a void. It should never feel like a constricting interior space, that's the visual challenge: even though it's architectural, it should make you feel it's a landscape. It's a restricted space, but one within infinity. I think that's appropriate.

The technical rehearsal continues, but soon hits a major problem with the moon. This is supposed to emerge slowly and silently from behind two panels which slide open above and below it. But it's proving difficult to coordinate the moon's rise, its colour, its gradual brightening, and the opening of the panels, which are also very noisy. After half an hour of frustrating attempts to find a solution, Kevin suggests they work on it overnight and test it again before tomorrow's dress rehearsal.

It's illuminating to watch how the four actors behave during the many stoppages that the technical rehearsal inevitably entails. Alan's preoccupation is with his bowler hat, which he continues to spin up into the air in the hope of landing it smoothly on his head: the success rate for this trick has now increased to about 50 per cent. James' tendency is to pace up and down; Terence remains in one place, apparently deep in thought; Richard chooses to practise his facial and other physical movements.

The rehearsal continues into the evening. One matter that needs resolving is the issue of the sound effects linked to Pozzo and Lucky's entrances and exits. The recorded whip heralding their arrival sounds too much like a circus whip, while the sound used for their fall offstage at their first exit doesn't have the right tone. Gregory Clarke offers Peter various possibilities and levels, and before long they find the right ones.

As they break for the night, Gregory explains his approach to the sound design.

Technically it's not an enormous challenge. But I've found this on simple shows, that it throws what you do into very sharp relief. This is especially true for a play like this, which is conceptually very different from most ones I've worked on.

Achieving the sound effects is not difficult; building them is the tricky bit. At this stage the challenge is to find something that Peter will accept. The more I work with him, the more I know how to read exactly what he wants. He's a fairly difficult person to read if you just take things on the surface, so you have to find those little words that tell you what he wants. He gave it to me fairly early on this time – so there's an offstage world and an onstage world.

We're talking about things that are very simple, such as people falling over and picking themselves up. If you pick yourself up off a hard wooden floor, then it doesn't really make any noise, even with Lucky's bags. So it's about finding a way to tighten those little moments that happen offstage, without making them comic. And making sure also, which is the continuing pressure on sound designers, that the audience knows exactly what's happening as soon as they hear it, particularly when there's no visual clue as to what's going on.

What I did was record a whole canvas of different sound effects, of the bags that we're using being picked up and thrown about with other pieces of luggage. At this stage I know what's going to work and I know we've got to change things a little sonically. I'll need to manipulate the material I have, or use different bits of it.

Tuesday 16 August

The technical rehearsal resumes in the morning. Once again the moon proves troublesome. 'There's always a problem, always, every time I do the play,' Peter mutters. The panels now slide quietly, but the timing and positioning of the moon are still awry. They spend another half hour trying to fix it, and eventually find a solution.

This time a real Boy comes in with the news from *chez* Godot. It's a disturbing scene now that the young actor is included, and he handles it with impressive assurance and timing. Since there are two boys alternating the part, it's necessary to do their scenes twice. First up is Brixton Hamilton, who is confident and looks angelic, but is not always audible. Cordelia on Peter's behalf asks him to play it again, and after two more attempts he achieves what they want. The second boy, Jack Lawrence, who is rather more bucolic looking, has a stronger voice, and projects it perfectly well. Peter is satisfied, but suggests the Boy's costume should suggest more of a farm image than a period one. He also feels that, while the other costumes are conveying the right impression, those of Vladimir and Estragon could do with a bit more 'distressing'.

A perfectionist to the end, he takes advantage of the stoppages to give small notes to the actors – 'Terry, remember you're blind when you take the whip' – or to remind them of word inflections – 'Things have *changed* around here – that's the emphasis, James.' He also finds the odd moment to take pictures of the action with his newly acquired camera.

Finally the technical rehearsal is over. For the actors it's been a long haul. In their dressing-rooms during the lunch break, while they prepare for the afternoon's dress rehearsal, I catch their latest thoughts (though not Terence's, as he's taking a nap).

JAMES: I quite like technical rehearsals, because you can start to feel your way around things, and find the bumps and the holes. Today has been interesting. The lovely thing is that with the theatricality of the piece, we have to play out front, and this is a theatre which is so obviously designed for you to do that, it's reassuring. But I think the acoustics are a bit seductive. I was in a few weeks ago to see another play, and they were not quite as good as people think they are. But the costumes are very fine, and I like the fact that my trousers are specially made by a tailor, and then distressed.

RICHARD: It's been brilliant getting on to the stage, and seeing everyone in their costumes. Some actors don't like all the technical side, but I love it, having the time to watch the others putting their roles together. It brings home the reality of the play, watching the characters come to life. It really gets your mind into focus, looking out into that darkness and imagining three hundred people sitting out there. It's always much easier to inhabit the world of the play once you get on stage. The acoustics seem lovely, and the costumes are excellent: just looking down and seeing the complete deterioration in my clothes helps me a lot. And the hotter I am, and the more I slather, the better it is for me. Peter said, Don't kill yourself, but I like to push myself as much as possible.

ALAN: The acoustics are excellent, it's my favourite theatre in that respect: it's a perfect Georgian shape, and a perfect size. Getting all the costumes helps to give you the shape and appearance of the play – although I find it a little ridiculous that our trousers are tailor made, and then specially torn and shredded. But they're well done. And it's good being on the stage and knowing you have to fill the whole auditorium. After six weeks in the rehearsal room, we need that extra dimension. It's also nice because one begins to think, Oh, this is a real show now, we're not just mucking about in a rehearsal room.

Afternoon. 'House lights down... Curtain up.' The dress rehearsal begins, disturbed only slightly by the sound of Nobby Clark's camera as he moves around the stalls taking more publicity photographs. It's a good performance: there are no major technical problems, and the actors have found a new mettle in their playing. I notice for the first time how well James uses his eyes, how Alan shifts so very expertly from anger to humour, how Terence manages to make Pozzo's more tender moments convincing, and how Richard achieves an extraordinary level of concentration when he's not part of the action.

Afterwards Peter talks to the actors at the front of the stalls. 'That was magnificent, absolutely terrific,' he says. 'The Pozzo and Lucky scenes were excruciating and nerve-wracking, the pain was wonderful. James and Alan, you are so responsive to each other, I think you may find it quite difficult at first to let the audience in. But it's more than ready for an audience. I have no idea how they're going to

14 From Max Wall to the Old Vic

'Beckett will be unique for generations to come'
– Actor/playwright Colin Welland

In 1979, while director of the National Theatre, Peter Hall tried to persuade Lindsay Anderson to direct *Waiting for Godot*. Anderson declined the invitation, arguing that the play needed to be performed by clowns, and that apart from Max Wall, England didn't breed such people. Within a year Wall, now seventy-three, was playing Vladimir in Manchester, and the following year in London.

The last of the old music-hall comedians, famed for his elastic face and matchstick legs, Wall already had a track-record in modern theatre. In the 1960s he had played in Alfred Jarry's controversial *Ubu Roi* at the Royal Court, and later appeared in Osborne's *The Entertainer* as Archie Rice and in Pinter's *The Caretaker*. His role in *Waiting for Godot* came about quite by accident. He had previously recorded scenes from it for the Open University, playing Vladimir to Leo McKern's Estragon. The actor Trevor Peacock, who was a friend, one day heard him quote a line, and asked if he had ever thought of doing the complete version on stage. 'Chance would be a fine thing,' Wall replied. Peacock contacted Braham Murray, for whom he had played Estragon in an earlier production, and Murray immediately agreed to direct the two of them at the Royal Exchange.

As a theatre in the round, with entrances at all four corners, the Royal Exchange provided a good setting for Vladimir and Estragon, who were literally at a crossroads, uncertain which way to go. 'It was a very potent image,' Murray recalled. 'In rehearsals I pursued the line that Vladimir was the head and Estragon the body, and concentrated on the bond between them. The clowning grew organically out of that. But I also wanted to get a balance between the tragedy and the comedy: if you can get those two elements right, the play works.'

The cast was completed by Wolfe Morris as Pozzo and Gary Waldhorn as Lucky. Rehearsals were slow to get going, especially in the afternoons, as Wall tended to consume too much Guinness at lunch time. One day he simply vanished from rehearsals, and Peacock found him in the pub. After four days they reached a crisis, as Murray remembers: 'In the middle of a rehearsal Max suddenly stopped and said: "That's it! You'll have to re-cast me. You obviously don't like what I'm doing." I said: "What ever makes you think that?" "Because there's nothing on your boat race (face)," he replied. So I said: "Well, I laughed the first time, but it's not quite the same when you hear the words again and again." "And another thing," he went on, "you keep on stopping me!" I said: "But that's what we do in rehearsals." And he replied: "I don't want to stop, I want to learn the lines!"'

Murray told Peacock he would concentrate all his notes on him, if necessary 'tearing him apart', in the hope that Wall would listen and take some of the notes on board himself. The plan worked, the play opened to great acclaim and full houses, both in Manchester and when it transferred to the Roundhouse in London. 'It was the most enjoyable play I've ever been in,' Peacock says. 'It's the human predicament exactly; it's got more happening in it than most other plays. And Max was wonderful: when you looked at him you saw the clown at first, but then the lonely, desperate, defiant human being.' Flushed with success, Wall asked Murray what he thought of the idea of him playing King Lear. 'I thought, oh God!' Murray recalls. 'So I told him that at one point he had to carry Cordelia. "Oh well," he said, "I don't think I'll do it then."'

Four years earlier Beckett had paid a visit to the newly built National Theatre, and talked to Hall about a new production. 'He wants us to do *Waiting for Godot* in the Olivier,' Hall wrote in his diary. 'I begged him to do the production himself. He says he can't face it again. He is seventy, and any energy he has must be used on writing.'

Two years later Beckett gave the same answer to Harold Pinter, who had also raised the idea of him directing the play at the National. Hall then decided to do it himself. The production was put into the Olivier schedule – and then cancelled, because Hall was offered Peter Shaffer's new play *Amadeus*, but only on condition that he stage it immediately. Finally, in 1987, Hall persuaded one of his associate directors, Michael Rudman, to mount a production.

Rudman was not particularly enthusiastic. He had been to a reading of the play in America when he was at university, and had not liked it; later he had walked out of a production in another university. But once he got into rehearsal he found himself totally fascinated. Before starting work he went to see Beckett in Paris. Despite his famous reluctance to answer questions about the play, Beckett, now eighty-one, was forthcoming on a few points. When Rudman asked him if Pozzo really owned the land, he replied that 'Pozzo is a bluff', and is 'always trying to make an impression'. Beckett admitted that he liked it best when his words were spoken by Irish actors, because their way of speaking 'enabled them to separate syllables'. But he also made it clear that he was opposed to actors trying to pin down the offstage or past life of their characters. After they had talked for more than an hour, Rudman apologised for tiring him. Beckett replied in true Estragon style: 'I would have got tired anyway.'

It was Rudman's intention to do a naturalistic production, but he realised from their discussion that Beckett was keen for the movement to be stylised, with an element of mime. 'In fact I think he wanted it done exactly as he'd done it at the Schiller Theatre – and I mean exactly,' he says. 'So at his suggestion we brought in as an adviser his assistant on that production, Walter Asmus. Although he was very sweet, and seemed to like what we were doing, we more or less ignored him. After all, we couldn't just repeat the Schiller production; that's not how directors work.'

The cast was an all-English one. Alec McCowen was Vladimir and John Alderton played Estragon, and they were supported by Colin Welland as Pozzo and Peter Wight playing Lucky. Rudman's aim, he told the actors, was to make the play 'extremely real, very funny and savagely upsetting'. For McCowen, working on it was a revelation: 'Although I disliked it when I first saw it, when I came to read it, it made sense, and I loved acting in it. Rehearsing it was very different from working on other plays. Vladimir and Estragon are a wonderful double-act, but the relationship between them is not defined, so you have to bring that to the play yourself. Fortunately, John and I got on very well.' Welland was already a fan of the play, having seen the 1964 Royal Court production: 'As we rehearsed it became more and more interesting, way beyond anything I had experienced before,' he remembers. 'The language is so rich, and so enjoyable to speak. But I found my part difficult to learn. Normally you can relate your lines to a physical action, but Pozzo is not playing off anyone, he just sits there eating and drinking, ranting and complaining.'

The actors clearly ignored Beckett's stricture about researching their characters' biographies. Wight, daunted by Lucky's speech, was concerned at the absence of hard information about his life: he found the clues to be 'of a tantalising nature', and described himself as 'half a biographer, tracking down details about Lucky's life, and half a novelist, imagining the full implications of these elusive details'. Alderton meanwhile took a highly unusual step in researching his part. Having noted down Estragon's characteristics, he took them to a psychoanalyst, who had agreed to treat his notes as if they related to a real person. He described Estragon as a classic case of chronic depression.

Two outside events impinged on the company's work during rehearsals: Rudman's son was born, and McCowen's partner died. Rudman recalls: 'Alec and I looked at each other one day, and thought, "I see now what this play is about, it's about life and death." After that I became obsessed with how wonderful it was.' For McCowen the effect of the play on him was unexpected: 'I found it very helpful, it was a great comfort,' he says. 'It suddenly made death seem more like a comedy than a tragedy.'

Directing the play removed all Rudman's doubts about its quality. 'Beckett, intentionally I think, makes the audience uncomfortable, and this is quite off-putting at the beginning. But then you realise this is part of a process, in which he draws you in and then pushes you away, and that is the fascination.' The production was generally well received. But three weeks into the run there was an accident. As Welland made an entrance he fell, twisted his knee, and tore the ligaments. Although he got through the performance, he had to leave the production, and was replaced by Terence Rigby.

In 1991 the play had its first West End performance in thirty-five years, when the comedians Rik Mayall and Adrian Edmondson starred in Les Blair's production at the Queen's, with a set designed by Derek Jarman. 'I have always been drawn to Beckett,' Mayall said during rehearsals. 'I like the simplicity. I like the honesty. I like the vulgarity, the violence.' He and Edmondson promised to come up with a very traditional version, with only minor changes to the text and stage directions. But Paul Taylor of the *Independent* felt they 'turned the play into a game of complicity with their fans and so destroyed any sense of the characters' isolation'.

In 1997 Hall returned to *Waiting for Godot*, staging it as part of his repertory season at the Old Vic. The cast was a starry one, with Alan Howard as Vladimir, Ben Kingsley playing Estragon, and Denis Quilley and Greg Hicks as Pozzo and Lucky. Hall deliberately avoided what he saw as the errors of his first production. In the interim he had seen Beckett's own production, both in Berlin and London. 'The production is quite, quite beautiful. It revived my faith in theatre,' he wrote in his diary, after seeing it at the Royal Court in 1976. 'Absolute precision, clarity, hardness. No sentimentality, no indulgence, no pretension.'

So for his second production there was no music, no clutter, not even a road or a mound in William Dudley's set: simply a bare stage with a tree and a rock. 'In trying to direct the play again, I'm once more astounded by its precision,' he observed during rehearsals. 'It has the clarity and the simplicity of the greatest art, such as the second act of *The Marriage of Figaro* or the whole of *A Midsummer Night's Dream*. It knows exactly what it's doing and how to accomplish it. We now have the benefit of all Beckett's later thoughts, all the tiny cuts and additions made for various productions. There is nothing remaining that is unclear, nothing that is pretentious, nothing finally baffling. It no longer seems obscure.'

Despite Beckett's views on actors searching for biographical details, Hall used improvisation to help them expand their knowledge of their characters. Bearing in mind Beckett's wartime experiences, when he and Suzanne were fleeing Paris and hiding from the Germans, he encouraged the cast to improvise scenes about being dispossessed, being on the run, and living in the open. This time he encouraged the actors to adopt light Irish accents, observing that 'the Anglo-Irish lilt releases the rhythm of the text like nothing else'. The comedy was brought out more strongly, and audiences were amused rather than bemused.

The production garnered rave notices. The critics noted that the play had become an accepted classic, and that Hall could now, as Michael Coveney put it in the *Daily Mail*, 'confidently allow it to breathe as a comedy'. Nicholas de Jongh in the *Evening Standard* wrote: 'How dateless, how timeless and how disturbingly fresh *Waiting for Godot* seems in Peter Hall's lucid new production.' Hall underlined this when he noted how young people coming to the Old Vic seemed to have no problem with the play. 'They wondered what all the fuss had been about. It was perfectly clear to them that it was about a couple of people waiting and trying to work out certain things about life.' Most critics thought the production both moving and funny, though some felt it was not sufficiently bleak or nightmarish, that it lacked a certain quality of desperation and anguish. Looking back now, Hall feels that certain elements were missing. 'I think the production was probably a tiny bit too cosy, possibly a little warm-hearted, not quite abrasive enough.'

He decided to stage the play again the following year, with a completely new cast. This time Julian Glover and Alan Dobie were Vladimir and Estragon, while Pozzo and Lucky were played by Terence Rigby and Struan Rodger. Hall had moved to the Piccadilly after the collapse of his season at the Old Vic, which the owner Ed Mirvish had decided to sell. The production alternated in repertoire with Molière's *Le Misanthrope*. Once again the play received excellent reviews, one or two critics putting it on a par with Beckett's own production in Berlin.

Although the set was again a minimal one, with a different company Hall started afresh. 'Peter never brings any baggage with him,' Alan Dobie says. 'Even when he's redoing a play, he always starts from scratch, as though he's forgotten it. So you always get a feeling that you are starting from the beginning.' For some of the cast, though, the rehearsal period was a very difficult one. Struan Rodger found huge problems in learning Lucky's speech. 'It was one of the hardest things I've ever had to do,' he remembers. 'Peter initially left me to my own devices, saying learn it first, and then we'll do it. It felt as if we were all on the top of a ski slope, and then the others went ahead on the piste, and I had to go off from a ski jump in order to catch them up. So I was a bit rocky to start with.'

Julian Glover also found rehearsals a painful experience: 'I was in despair about learning the lines, I used to come home every night almost in tears,' he remembers. 'I simply don't believe any actor who says that it's enjoyable to play in *Godot*. They're either telling lies or deluding themselves. It's a nightmare to play, because it's so precise, and nothing to do with true communication, as it's mainly a mechanical exercise. Peter was very helpful and encouraging, he thought we were a good mix, and I think he knew we were going to pull it off. He was very firm about the length of the pauses and silences, which are difficult to accommo-

119

date as an actor if you're trying to be natural. When it came to the performances, I stood there each time by the tree at the start of the show, my heart filled with foreboding. I never looked forward to it – and yet in the end it was a very satisfying experience.'

Looking back seven years later, Hall felt that it was a definite improvement on the previous production. 'I think it was much more on the road to where we should have been going.'

15 Finding an Audience

Tuesday 16 August

In the evening the Bath audience stream in to the elegant auditorium of the Theatre Royal, with its cream walls traced with gold, its large glass chandelier hanging above the stalls, and its traditional deep red curtain. Soon every seat is full as they wait for the first preview to begin. Smartly and conventionally dressed, they seem like a typical middle-class audience. Although I see a few young people here and there, and even a couple of boys who can't be more than ten, the large majority would certainly have been alive when *Waiting for Godot* opened in London fifty years ago. How will they react to a piece of theatre that has become a classic in their lifetime?

The opening minutes are greeted in what feels like a respectful silence. The laughs, when they come, are tentative. James and Alan are doing everything right, but the audience don't yet seem fully engaged. Then Pozzo and Lucky arrive, and suddenly they are gripped. Terence is characteristically terrifying, while Richard delivers his big speech with his usual power and clarity: as he falls to the ground at the end the audience are palpably stunned. The rest of the act goes smoothly – until, a couple of minutes before the end, as the moon is about to rise, the curtain suddenly begins to fall, and the house lights start to come up. It's a horrible moment, but the mistake is immediately corrected, and James and Alan carry on calmly until the curtain falls again, this time at the right moment.

As the audience return for the second act, a woman in the row behind me says: 'That slave was so disturbing, I wanted to run out of the theatre.' But she didn't; indeed no one seems to have left. No walk outs, no yawns or groans, no shouting back at the actors on lines such as 'I've been better entertained' or 'It's awful'. Although the play clearly stirs up all kinds of emotions, anger or boredom don't appear to be among them. At the end, as the light fades out on Vladimir and Estragon, still waiting in the bleak landscape, the audience applaud with obvious approval, and at length.

A few minutes later, in the now almost empty stalls, Peter talks briefly with the production team. It was, he says, a very good show for a first preview, and everyone is to be congratulated. There's a brief discussion about the miscued curtain, which seems to have been caused by a computer programming error, for which the culprit apologises. 'I don't mind people making mistakes and saying sorry,' Peter says, 'as long as we know what went wrong – and it doesn't happen again.'

He'll be giving the actors their notes in the morning. Meanwhile he offers me some instant thoughts on the performance.

On the whole it was very good tonight. I think the actors were slightly nervous and tight, which they always are on these occasions. They pushed it a tiny bit too much, which had the effect of pushing the audience slightly away from them. But I thought they were very, very attentive. I'd like them to have laughed more early on, but it always takes a little while to produce that effect. The feeling was that they'd come to see a modern classic, and they must attend, and work it out. They were rapt, their attention was fantastic. I didn't observe anyone leaving. Nobody said, when Terence came back in the second act, I wish the fat one would go away, which was said to Peter Bull during the first production. All those bombs that Beckett put in, none of them got a raucous response, they just got laughs.

I think the mood at the beginning was just a little too despairing, that was a slight criticism. But nothing else was substantially off, except the scene where they discuss whether to help Pozzo or not. That was not heartless enough, but then I suppose audiences push actors towards sympathy. Overall they really did a magnificent job. They're a wonderful cast, and they know what's behind the play.

Thursday 25 August

There have been five further previews since the first one nine days ago. According to Peter, the actors were much more relaxed on the second preview night, both emotionally and physically, and the audience were much more comfortable about laughing. Since then, he feels, the production has improved with each performance. But now it's press night – or rather press afternoon, since *Waiting for Godot* and *You Never Can Tell* are being staged on the same day for the convenience of the London-based critics, and the Shaw play is scheduled for this evening.

The audience settles as the curtain rises. The beginning is now slower, which feels better, and the audience more responsive, their laughter more uninhibited. I notice various changes. Richard now has a whiter face and blacker eyes, which make Lucky seem a more desperate case than ever. Terence has speeded up one or two speeches that were too slow, and is finding a greater variety of emotion for Pozzo. James' despair is deeper, especially at the end, while Alan, who had feared his performance was becoming too bleak, has raised Estragon's mischief level a notch or two.

The moon functions perfectly, and the curtain rises and falls on cue. A few new pieces of business have been added, such as Vladimir clutching Estragon's smelly boot to his heart, which gives greater emphasis to their camaraderie. Lucky's speech this time gets a round of applause, which it apparently has done since the second performance. The pauses are more sustained, and so more potent, creating both greater tension and a stronger sense of the characters' desperate situation.

Afterwards, in an empty auditorium, Peter summons up his immediate thoughts.

This opening was certainly not as nerve-racking and as tense an experience for me as the one fifty years ago at the Arts.

But it was still quite alarming, because this is the best cast I've ever had, and I wanted them to be so good. Happily, they were terrific.

Terence's Pozzo had a kind of Alice in Wonderland madness about it, he seemed to be utterly real, and yet utterly mad. He's taken the point of self-regard and self-concern and selfishness to a point where nothing seems to exist except him, everything he talks about is related to him. Now if you look at the text that's the way it is. But I've never seen an actor bring that off so well. Usually it's more of a bullying, fascist-like performance. His moods are extremely changeable, he moves wonderfully well from the angry and the resentful, the fascist, to the courteous land-owner, dropping by to give the peasants a brace of rabbits.

Richard was I think superb. He gave you a sense of Lucky's inner life, his inner torment, and what that poor mangled head must be doing. He made great sense of the big speech by endorsing its nonsense – it's like the computer's gone wrong, and it just tells you all the words that have ever been told. His physical life as an actor was extraordinary, and it was a remarkable performance.

Alan and James are a lovely pair, who have learnt to act together like a couple of expert jazz players. There was something about Alan's performance that was very endearing, particularly when he was being impossible, shouting and carrying on like a naughty child. And there was something extremely disturbing and touching about the way James did the final section, being a man alone in space, expressing the panic of the intellectual whose reason doesn't serve him after all. It was very brilliant. I think he is a great actor, because he has that everyman quality. All great actors carry with them this quality: when they walk on the stage they do so for *us*, when you see them suffer, when you see them deranged, they're doing it for us, and in a sense *as* us. I think James, who is an extremely good actor, found a sense of everyman in the last twenty minutes of the play which I shall find difficult to forget.

At the party that evening there's a feeling of deep satisfaction, a general sense that the actors have given of their best. It now remains to see if the critics agree.

16 The Godot Effect

'He was an inspiration to all writers, and certainly was to me' – Harold Pinter

For the older, established playwrights such as Noël Coward and Terence Rattigan, masters of the well-made play, *Waiting for Godot* was an unwelcome arrival on the London theatre scene. Their horrified reactions show how subversive the play was, and how against all the received wisdom about dramatic form and content.

Having seen Hall's 1955 production at the Criterion, Rattigan wrote an article in the *New Statesman* headed 'Aunt Edna Waits for Godot', in which he filtered his dismay and disapproval through a fictitious aunt, supposedly representing the ordinary theatregoer. 'How could I like the play, seeing that Mr Samuel Beckett plainly hates me so much that he's refused point blank to give me a play at all?' Aunt Edna asks her nephew. 'I suppose he's a highbrow, but even a middlebrow like myself could have told him that a really good play had to be on two levels, an upper one, which I suppose you'd call symbolical, and a lower one, which is based on story and character. By writing on the upper level alone, all Mr Beckett has done is to produce one of those things that thirty years ago we used to call Experimental Drama.'

By 1960 the play's reputation was more secure, a fact which infuriated Coward, who disliked it intensely: 'In my considered opinion it is pretentious gibberish, without any claim to importance whatsoever,' he wrote in his diary in August of that year. 'It is nothing but phoney surrealism with occasional references to Christ and mankind. It has no form, no basic philosophy and absolutely no lucidity… It's just a waste of everybody's time, and it made me ashamed to think that such balls could be taken seriously for a moment.'

Many of the new generation of playwrights emerging in the 1950s and 1960s did indeed take it seriously. In America Beckett's influence was to be seen in Edward Albee's absurdist one-act play *The Zoo Story*, in which two men struggle for control of a park bench; in David Mamet's first play *Duck Variations*, a rambling conversation between two old men; and in Sam Shepard's *Cowboys #2 – Waiting for Godot* was the first play Shepard remembered reading. In Britain the play most obviously made its mark on the work of Harold Pinter and Tom Stoppard. But it was also visible elsewhere, for example in the plays of Athol Fugard in South Africa, and the work of the Czech playwright Václav Havel. *Waiting for Godot* enabled these and other writers to break free from the conventions of plot and character, to experiment with non-realistic dialogue, to use unlocalised settings, and to play games with the elements of time and space. As Ronald Harwood puts it: 'It helped to change not just the face of theatre, but also its heart and soul. It blew fresh air into the theatre, and made possible all that was to follow at the Royal Court.'

Pinter was probably the playwright most immediately affected by Beckett's works. An early fan of the novels, he was fascinated by *Waiting for Godot*, which he saw during its West End run in 1955. The two men became friends in 1960, and thereafter Pinter sent Beckett the typescript of each of his plays, about which Beckett would make brief but pertinent comments. 'He didn't admit any frontiers to his writing,' Pinter observed approvingly. 'He was fearless in his life and in his art.' In 1970 he described Beckett as 'the greatest writer of our time'.

Pinter was twenty-two, and an actor touring Ireland with Anew McMaster's company, when he first discovered Beckett's work in 1953. He read an extract from his novel *Murphy* in a poetry magazine, and was stunned by it. 'I suddenly felt that what his writing was doing was walking through a mirror into the other side of the world which was, in fact, the real world,' he remembered. On return-ing to London he tracked down a copy of the novel, then read all Beckett's postwar work. The appeal was instant. Pinter later wrote: 'The further he goes the more good it does me. I don't want philosophies, tracts, dogmas, creeds, way outs, truths, answers, nothing from the bargain basement. He is the most courageous, remorseless writer going, and the more he grinds my nose in the shit the more I am grateful to him.'

Pinter was also in Ireland two years later when he heard that Hall's production of *Waiting for Godot* was opening in London. He wrote to Hall expressing his interest in the play, and tried to get hold of a copy of the text. His friend Mick Goldstein saw the production and wrote to him about it. 'Your letter does make me gnash my teeth that I can't see it,' Pinter replied. 'It sounds a fascinating play.' He went on to argue at length with his friend, who clearly thought the play superficial, and possibly a joke. Pinter, already a huge fan of Beckett's novels, demurred. 'From what I know of Beckett I don't see how *Waiting for Godot* could be a joke, even a good one,' he wrote. Humorous and argumentative, the letter (reproduced in full in Appendix 1) provides a fascinating early glimpse of Pinter's mind, and his thoughts on the question of whether a playwright has a responsibility to explain his work: 'Is it Beckett's business to answer questions he himself poses? I do not see that. For the good of the play you suggest? But what is a good play? Does it keep you in your seat?' Back in London, he went to see the play at the Criterion, and was shocked when at the end a man stood up and described the play as 'the greatest rubbish I've ever seen'.

Just like *Waiting for Godot*, Pinter's early plays were initially greeted with derision, irritation or incomprehension, and described as obscure and enigmatic. The plays provided for most people in the audience a totally new theatrical experience. When Pinter began to make his mark as a playwright, critics and others were quick to link him with Beckett and *Waiting for Godot*. It was noted that *The Dumb Waiter*, written in 1957, was about two men waiting in a basement, apparently at the mercy of a higher authority.

The critic Michael Billington suggested: 'You can interpret it as an absurdist comedy – a kind of *Godot* in Birmingham – about two men passing the time in a universe without meaning or purpose.' When *The Birthday Party* was first staged, and savaged by the critics, it was linked to what one described as 'the school of random dottiness derived from Beckett and Ionesco'. And when *The Caretaker* – later described as '*Waiting for Godot* set in the Chiswick High Road' – was an instant success in 1960, Davies the tramp and Aston, paralysed in inaction, were compared with Vladimir and Estragon. Some of Pinter's later plays, such as *No Man's Land*, *Silence* and *Landscape*, were also felt to be influenced by Beckett's works.

The most obvious debt Pinter owes to Beckett is a technical one. With his deep-seated concern for the rhythm of *Waiting for Godot*, Beckett used the stage directions to indicate different kinds of pauses and silences. This technique was adopted by Pinter: in the plays of both men the directions become as much a part of the text as the words spoken by the actors. Their plays also share a mysterious quality, and often deal among other matters with a failure of the characters to communicate. Yet whatever the debt and the influence, Pinter's early plays are in the end very different from Beckett's, being generally more social and specific, rooted in a recognisable reality, and concerned with individual psychology, while Beckett's are more obviously metaphorical and universal.

Stoppard is another playwright who has been influenced by Beckett, as well as by writers as diverse as Eliot, Pirandello and Kafka. For him, *Waiting for Godot* 'liberated something for anybody writing plays'. Like Pinter, he was also impressed by the novels: 'I find Beckett deliciously funny in the way that he qualifies everything as he goes along, reduces, refines and dismantles. When I read it I love it.' *Waiting for Godot* he saw as 'a shocking event, because it completely redefined the minima of a valid theatrical transaction. Up until then, to have a play at all you had to have x, you couldn't have a tenth of x and have a play.'

Stoppard first saw *Waiting for Godot* at the Bristol Old Vic in 1957, when he was a twenty-year-old journalist working in the city. The production starred Peter O'Toole at the very beginning of his career. 'It remains the one I remember most clearly, although perhaps this is true of everyone's first Godot,' he says, nearly fifty years on. 'All four performances remain definitive for me.' The influence was clearly discernible in his first one-act play *The Gamblers*, a two-hander involving a Prisoner and a Jailer, who discuss religion, philosophy and death, and at times indulge in the kind of cross-talk favoured by Vladimir and Estragon. Stoppard later labelled the play '*Waiting for Godot* in the Condemned Cell'. But it was *Rosencrantz and Guildernstern Are Dead*, the play which made him an overnight success, that showed most strikingly how he had absorbed Beckett's revolutionary work. Infused with the spirit of *Godot*, it might reasonably have been called 'Waiting for Hamlet'.

'Prufrock and Beckett are the two syringes of my diet, my arterial system,' Stoppard observed at the time. Inspired by Eliot's celebrated poem ('No! I am not Prince Hamlet, nor was meant to be;/Am an attendant lord...'), and centring on Hamlet's two courtier friends, who linger offstage away from Shakespeare's main action and debate matters of life, death, probability and much else, his play shares with Beckett's the image of two lost souls waiting for something to happen – as Guildernstern puts it, 'we move idly towards eternity, without possibility of reprieve or hope of explanation'. The setting of the action, an empty landscape, is also reminiscent of Beckett's play, as is the abundance of questions, and the lack of certain answers. Stoppard also makes use of cross-talk and contradiction, and what he has described as 'the Beckett joke', which consists of 'confident statement followed by immediate refutation'. But the homage goes further: Rosencrantz and Guildernstern actually quote – or rather misquote – phrases from *Waiting for Godot*.

Stoppard's work soon broadened out, moving away from its absurdist beginnings to explore with dazzling wit questions of science, literary biography, journalism and revolutionary politics. In his third full-length play, *Jumpers*, he made explicit his debt to Beckett, allowing George the moral philosopher to parody Vladimir's speech about birth and death, and to end: 'Wam, bam, thank you Sam.' But like most playwrights, he wearied of people asking him which writers had influenced his work. When someone asked him at a Platform session at the National Theatre in 1993 about his debt to Beckett, he responded succinctly: 'I paid it back.'

The South African playwright Athol Fugard is another who has expressed his admiration of Beckett. Like the Irishman's plays, his often emphasise the absurdity of life, though they are much more embedded in the social and political realities of his country. *Boesman and Lena*, considered the best full-length play of his apprenticeship, clearly owed a substantial debt to *Waiting for Godot*. Written in 1968, it managed to encapsulate the tragic conditions of apartheid South Africa. The story concerns a Coloured man and woman who are forced by the state's oppressive laws to trek into the countryside from their shantytown, which is being bulldozed to make room for homes for the White population. Barefoot and in rags, a tragic bickering couple, stuck in a bleak landscape and bound together in mutual misery, Boesman and Lena are strongly reminiscent of Vladimir and Estragon.

In 1983 the Czech playwright Václav Havel wrote to Beckett: 'I have been immensely influenced by you as a human being, and in a way as a writer too.' He explained that 'during the dark fifties when I was sixteen or eighteen years of age, in a country where there was virtually no cultural or other contacts with the outside world, luckily I had the opportunity to read *Waiting for Godot*.' Havel's early absurdist plays certainly showed that influence. Later, after he had been imprisoned for his dissident views and activities, he had reason to be personally grateful to Beckett. Appalled to learn that Havel had been forbidden to write as part of his punishment for protesting against the abuse of human rights in Czechoslovakia, Beckett wrote a powerful, uncharacteristically political play called *Catastrophe*, and dedicated it to Havel. Released the following year, Havel wrote his short play *Mistake* as a response.

A year after *Waiting for Godot* burst on the London scene, *Look Back in Anger* created a similar furore at the Royal Court. John Osborne's play brought a new kind of expression and voice into a theatre which, in Arthur Miller's words, was 'hermetically sealed off from reality'. It certainly created a seismic shift, opening the theatre up to a new breed of dramatists, including John Arden, Arnold Wesker, Ann Jellicoe, Willis Hall and Shelagh Delaney. Fifty years on it seems a very conventional play, and very much of its time. *Waiting for Godot*, on the other hand, has endured, its profundity increasingly recognised.

Two projects set up recently will help to keep its flame alive. The first is the Godot Company, established by John Calder and the actor Peter Marinker (see Appendix 3). The second is the ambitious *Beckett on Film* project, directed by Michael Lindsay-Hogg, which has put all nineteen of Beckett's theatre works on film. His version of *Waiting for Godot* uses the cast of the celebrated Gate production from Dublin, with Barry McGovern and Johnny Murphy as Vladimir and Estragon, and Stephen Brennan and Alan Stanford as Pozzo and Lucky.

In 2000 Fintan O'Toole wrote: 'The moral integrity and artistic authority of Beckett's response to the terror of his times makes him arguably the playwright of the twentieth century.' Widely acknowledged as a masterpiece, constantly played in colleges, schools and prisons as well as commercial theatres large and small, *Waiting for Godot* continues profoundly to affect writers, actors, directors and audiences worldwide.

17 Summing Up: The Actors, the Critic and the Director

Shortly after the run ended in Bath, the actors gave me their final thoughts about the play and the production.

James touched on the audience response: 'At the last performance it was standing room only, and we played to an audience that seemed rapt throughout, so we must have been doing something right. Audiences found it funny, which of course it is; but people have a notion that *Godot* is difficult and serious, so it was good to overcome that preconception.' Alan, while underlining the impossibility of being objective, had some reservations about the production: 'My sixth sense tells me that some niceness crept in, some sentiment or sympathy, whereas I like it hard and cruel. Life is cruel, giving birth is painful. I don't think anything about Beckett's writing is sentimental.'

While the actors generally felt the run was much too short, Terence would also have liked more rehearsal time. 'It's the kind of play that would benefit everyone if you rehearsed it for much longer, as there are endless mysteries to unravel. It was also a problem doing it in repertoire with the Shaw play, as it prevented you achieving the kind of rhythm you get from constant repetition.' Meanwhile Richard was still feeling the physical effects: 'Lucky was without doubt the most physically demanding part I've ever done. I spent nine weeks in a kind of shuddering spasm, my body is still recovering, and I'm still shaking. But it was a joy for me to catch flashes of Beckett's mind, and glimpse little pieces of humanity in its rawest, purest form. I'm still haunted by it, and I think I always will be.'

Finally I asked them what they had found most valuable in Peter's directing. For Alan, who had worked with him half a dozen times before, it was the fact that 'unlike so many directors nowadays, he never imposes any pre-conceived ideas on the proceedings, but allows the play to grow organically'. Terence pointed to his 'prolific talent', but also the production's 'excellent support team – I think of it as a team triumph'. Richard felt he had handled his work on Lucky's speech with sensitivity. 'He left me to find my own interpretation, which showed trust, and only spoke to me when he saw I needed guidance. When he did, his observations were incredibly precise.' James noted 'his ability, not necessarily found in all directors, to allow or encourage you to make a fool of yourself in rehearsal, which is terrific: it creates a useful freedom, and it also makes the work fun.'

By now all the daily, Sunday and weekly reviews had appeared. In striking contrast to those that greeted Peter's original production, they were almost uniformly excellent. The critics showered praise on performances and production alike, and only regretted that the play could not be seen in London.

Significantly, they took it as given that the play had become a classic, and needed no defending or explaining. 'Samuel Beckett's play is a masterpiece of world theatre, and there is nothing more to be done,' Michael Coveney announced in the *Observer*. In the *Daily Telegraph* Charles Spencer described Beckett's play as 'one of those inexhaustible classics that time can't tarnish', declaring that the story 'seems as fresh and resonant today as it ever did'. Admitting that when younger he had found Beckett's pessimism facile, he now thought the play 'true and uplifting rather than depressing and glib'; it was, he wrote, 'a work that transcends gloom', one that 'is more like a hymn to human endurance'. Meanwhile Michael Billington in the *Guardian* wrote: 'Sometimes Godot seems to be a philosophical comedy about the absurdity of existence. At other times it becomes a cry of rage at life's cruelty. But this version...becomes about human interdependence and our desperate need for company as we stumble through the void.'

The production was admired on several counts. Charles Spencer ended his review: 'This is a masterly production of a masterpiece, capturing all of Beckett's poetry and pity.' For Benedict Nightingale in *The Times*, 'pace, simplicity and subtlety' were the mark of the production: 'All in all, I can't imagine a much better salute to Beckett and *Godot*.' In the *Sunday Times* Victoria Segal, who thought the play 'as otherworldly as a chunk of moon rock, a fragment of something both familiar and wildly alien', concluded: 'Hall draws out that dreamlike quality with mesmerising force, shunning stunt casting or tricks for a beautifully clear production.' Michael Coveney called the production 'pitch perfect', stating that 'Hall exerts a magisterial control over the sad and funny back-chat in the void'; Alastair Macaulay in the *Financial Times* praised the director's 'classical regard for Beckett's phrasing, dynamics, sonorities'; while Georgina Brown in the *Mail on Sunday* noted: 'Hall sounds all the play's notes, the lyricism, the humour, the darkness, the light, the mystery. The result is as moving as it is exhilarating.'

The actors' performances were also widely admired. In the *Sunday Telegraph* Susan Irvine wrote: 'It is hard to imagine that Estragon and Vladimir were ever played with such surpassing ease as by Alan Dobie and James Laurenson. They clown with Beckett's words like a pair of master jugglers, while indulging in much physical clowning, an element brought to a comic peak in this production.' Victoria Segal called them 'a credible double act', while Charles Spencer noted the pair's 'beautiful performances… Laurenson's gentle, solicitous Vladimir contrasting sharply with Dobie's cussed, crabby Estragon'.

Richard Dormer's performance as Lucky received high approval ratings, as did his delivery of the Think. Susan Irvine called it 'astonishing', while Victoria Segal admired its display of 'a dizzying range and rhythm as he springs between voices, a human satellite receiving hundreds of messages at once'. He and Terence Rigby received several joint plaudits, notably from Charles Spencer, who described their performances as 'mesmerising', while Kate Bassett in the *Independent on Sunday* wrote: 'Rigby's patriarchal but crumpling Pozzo and Richard Dormer's enslaved Lucky are an unforgettable portrait of Victorian hierarchies crumbling before our eyes.'

Only two critics had reservations. In Benedict Nightingale's case they were relatively minor: he wondered if the cross-talk between Vladimir and Estragon sometimes became 'too quickfire', and whether Lucky's anguished monologue was 'too elaborate'. Kate Bassett, however, decided that it was 'hard to get hugely excited' about the production, and went on to criticise 'some over-reverential delivery of Beckett's bleak philosophising'.

A few days after the end of the run in Bath, I talked with Peter in his London home. He was understandably pleased with the excellent reviews.

> I've had notices in the past which have said, This is twaddle, it's full of pauses, and what does it mean? This time the critics *got* the play. They've cottoned on to the fact that if Beckett says one thing he might well mean another. And therefore they're slightly cagey about giving their own interpretation, which I don't think they should be, because their interpretation is valid like anyone else's. But it's very gratifying, when you've lived with a play for fifty years, to be told that you are hearing its music and its rhythm, and understanding its essential nature.

I asked him how he rated this production alongside his earlier ones, and what he thought the differences were.

> It was certainly the best Godot I've done, and I'm not sure it wasn't the best production I've done in Bath. To be immodest, by the eleventh and last performance on the Saturday afternoon, I felt it was as good as Sam's own one at the Schiller theatre in Berlin. I realise coming back to it that it's the play I know better than any other, including any of Shakespeare's. What the actors brought to it was extraordinary. It was painful to watch, because the comedy veered into painful situations and out again with such rapidity that you were almost frightened to go on participating in the play, because it was so terribly disturbing. But that abrasive-

ness, that harshness, allied to the humanity and the laughter, seems to me where the play resides. My job was to make the play as I think the man meant it, and I think I got nearer to it this time than I ever have before. That's why I'm proud of it.

My first production at the Arts was too scenic, it had lots of leaves on the tree, and little wisps of music, which I shudder to think of now. But I do know that it was genuinely and properly funny and touching, and got to the audience and made a lot of people cry. That doesn't happen if you've got it wrong. By the time I came back to it in 1997, I'd done other Beckett plays, and I knew Sam, so the Beckett aesthetic was part of me. I'd moved more into the purity of his theatre, I knew about his idea that less is more, so that on a bare stage you just need the one tree, and if you're really feeling extravagant you can have five leaves, but no more. But one thing has not changed. Partly because my being as a director is musical, and therefore more about sound and rhythm than it is perhaps about vision, I do know the tune of Beckett, his rhythm, his cadences. That got to me in 1995, and has continued to do so.

Remembering the hostile response his first production received half a century ago, I wondered what he made of the enormous enthusiasm of the Bath audience.

Bath took the play to its heart. I would never have predicted that, on a Wednesday afternoon in August with the sun beating down and a blue sky, people would be standing to watch *Waiting for Godot*, and others would be turned away in their hundreds from a midweek matinee. At the last performance on Saturday there were practically riots, among people who couldn't get in. Sam would have laughed extremely wryly. Clearly we were speaking to an audience that had heard us. And it seems there isn't now an audience that *wouldn't* be able to hear the play. Nobody came up to me and said, What does it mean? How dare you do this? – which they used to in the old days. The play has now become part of theatre life, but I hope it's also become part of our cultural being. In my mind it is a very great play. It's not an oddity or an aberration, it's an absolutely central metaphor about living. It's extraordinary how the play manages to say so much about death. It makes you cry and it makes you laugh, and I think you walk out knowing a little more about how you might deal with tomorrow.

Given the very limited run in Bath, I asked him if he might ever consider directing a fifth production.

We're going back to Bath for another season, so I hope if the actors are free we might be able to include this production in the repertoire. But if we can't, I still might do another one in three or four years' time. Coming back to it again only reinforces my view that it's one of the everlasting master-pieces of theatre.

Finally, I wondered if he believed that *Waiting for Godot* would still be performed in fifty years' time.

I have no doubt that it will, it's a landmark play histori-cally. But it won't be for that reason. The reason is that if it arrived on my desk now, unannounced, unheralded and unknown, as a new play, I wouldn't say to myself, What a Fifties play! Because it's completely up to date and up to the minute, it has its finger on our pulses, and I don't think you can say that of many plays, unless they are masterpieces. What do I mean by a masterpiece? A work that will speak to successive generations. I don't imagine it will be any easier to figure out who Godot is, or why he doesn't come, and I don't imagine it will be any easier to live a life with some-body else without bickering and quarrelling. But the play has enormous lessons for us. How are you to get through each day? Is it work? Is it sleep? Is it meditation? Is it fight-ing? How do you get through it, and what are you left with at the end of the day?

So it will be there. Lots of other plays won't be, because they will be of purely historical interest. *Waiting for Godot* on the other hand is like a great poem: it's eternal.

Sources

These books were especially valuable to me while I was investigating the stage history of *Waiting for Godot*:

Odette Aslan, *Roger Blin and Twentieth-Century Playwrights*, Cambridge University Press, 1988.

Deirdre Bair, *Samuel Beckett: A Biography*, Jonathan Cape, 1978.

David Bradby, *Beckett: Waiting for Godot*, Cambridge University Press, 2001.

Ruby Cohn (ed), *Beckett: Waiting for Godot: A Selection of Critical Essays*, Macmillan, 1987.

James Knowlson, *Damned to Fame: The Life of Samuel Beckett*, Bloomsbury, 1996.

The following books also proved useful:

Michael Billington, *The Life and Work of Harold Pinter*, Faber & Faber, 1996.

Peter Bull, *I Know the Face, but...*, Peter Davies, 1959.

Colin Chambers, *Peggy: The Life of Margaret Ramsay, Play Agent*, Nick Hern Books, 1997

Peter Hall, *Making an Exhibition of Myself*, Oberon Books, 1999.

Nicholas de Jongh, *Politics, Prudery and Perversions: The Censoring of the English Stage 1901–1968*, Methuen, 2000.

Stephen Fay, *Power Play: The Life and Times of Peter Hall*, Hodder & Stoughton, 1995.

Christopher Morash, *A History of Irish Theatre 1601–2000*, Cambridge University Press, 2002.

Ira Nadel, *Double Act: A Life of Tom Stoppard*, Methuen, 2002.

John Peter, *Vladimir's Carrot: Modern Drama and the Modern Imagination*, André Deutsch, 1987.

to hazard, an answer. In other words, surely the sole and necessary answer to the question is the play itself. The work is, must be, both things at the same time. Godot does not appear, Godot does not appear. Is that, or is it not, the crux of the matter? In that case, he does not appear and, in Beckett's point of view, does not appear. All I have to go on is what I can take from you and from the winds. Whether he appears or not, the tramps await him. Two things stated; absence and attendance. The question and answer in a nut. If the question was answered explicitly, the question would cease to exist, it would be consumed in the answer. There would be no impulse, no work, no play. In this matter, I take it, both exist as neighbours, mutually dependent and necessary, but distinct, at the same time as they may be so closely embraced to the point of non-recognition. I mean as to be unrecognisable one from the other. Anyway, I'm taking your word for it that the 'message' is a question. It isn't a statement containing both question and answer? You are in a position to know more about this than I do, and I would like to hear more. The point is that from all I've read of Beckett I can't quite see this message/question business. Of course he may have branched out. Both in he and Kafka, surely, you get all the questions and any answer you want, off any shelf, in any permutation, according to your taste and disposition, but I'd hesitate to say that I found one dominant question in these domains – except for the fact that there's always one dominant question behind any work of art, or it would not be born – X. Is birth a question? A question with a cast, or a twinkle in its eye. I prefer the term gut ache, a major irritation, a most stern and ruthless activity without question or answer, a three-card trick, a necessity. The necessity to what? The necessity to say. To say what? Whatever's to be said. What is to be said? Nothing is to be said, all is to be said. It is to be said. It is said. Some people say it better than others. Say what? What is to be said. Why? I ignore this question! So what do you mean superficial? That's what I want to know. Of course there's a twinkle in Beckett's eye. Do you want him without the twinkle? I can hardly believe that. You don't find the twinkle the canker? When then is the canker? He is not sincere about his message? What do you mean? I don't get that. I can't understand how such a question (of his sincerity) can arise. What do you think he is doing? Playing for safety? If there is one thing I can't see him doing, it's that. Perhaps you want him to put all his cards on the table when no bugger knows how many cards he's got in the first place, let alone how many he may be putting on any given table. From what I know of Beckett I don't see how *Waiting for Godot* could be a joke, even a good one. It may be a JOKE but it can't be a joke. I want to hear more about your findings. It sounds a fascinating play. I do hope I receive a copy.

Yours

Harold

Appendix 2
The Company, Bath 2005

Vladimir James Laurenson
Estragon Alan Dobie
Lucky Richard Dormer
Pozzo Terence Rigby
Boy Brixton Hamilton / Jack Lawrence

Director Peter Hall
Associate Director Cordelia Monsey
Set Designer Kevin Rigdon
Lighting Designer Peter Mumford
Costume Designers Kevin Rigdon / Trish Rigdon
Sound Designer Gregory Clarke
Costume Supervisor Joan Hughes
Company and Stage Manager Jerry Gunn
Deputy Stage Manager Donna Reeves
Assistant Stage Manager Juliet Earle Richards
Wardrobe Mistress Denny Evans

Appendix 3
The Godot Company

In 2002 John Calder, Beckett's publisher, and the actor Peter Marinker set up a cooperative called The Godot Company. With a dozen other actors, they perform *Waiting for Godot* and other Beckett plays in theatres, churches, schools and colleges, both in the UK and abroad.

In staging its productions the company closely follows Beckett's intentions. 'We are going very precisely by his stage directions,' John Calder says. 'Beckett knew exactly how he wanted things done, and we use his own notebooks, which are very precise. We've discovered that the closer you stick to his directions, the more the audiences get out of it. There's nothing obscure about Beckett. It's when new young directors try to put in ideas of their own that things go wrong and the audience get puzzled.'

The company also presents Beckett evenings at The Calder Bookshop, 51 The Cut, London SE1 8LP, telephone 020 7633 0599.

For further information go to: www.godotcompany.com

Index

Note: References to the chapters covering the 2005 Bath production are shown in **bold**.

Behind the Scenes

Journey of the Tall Horse: A Story of African Theatre
by Mervyn Millar

'A cast of characters so full of life that they take us by our cynical hands and lead us from our conditioned reality to a new universe of magic and illusion'
Sunday Independent

ISBN 1 84002 599 9   £15.99

Are You There, Crocodile? – Inventing Anton Chekhov
by Michael Pennington

'A classic depiction of theatre work at its most visionary' Simon Callow

ISBN 1 84002 458 5   £12.99   (paperback)
ISBN 1 84002 192 6   £19.99   (hardback)

NT At Work Series

Staging Greek Theatre: Peter Hall's Bacchai
by Jonathan Croall

ISBN 1 84002 463 1   £12.99

With the Rogue's Company: Henry IV at the National Theatre
by Bella Merlin

ISBN 1 84002 560 3   £12.99

The Art of Darkness: Staging the Philip Pullman Trilogy
by Robert Butler

'Daemons, cliff-ghasts, lovelorn witches, gyptians, harpies, armoured bears, soul-sucking spectres and tiny creatures riding dragonflies – the magical creations of writer Philip Pullman soared from page to stage yesterday in what could be the most spectacular theatre blockbuster ever. ' David Smith, *Observer*

ISBN 1 84002 414 3   £12.99

The Art of Darkness: The Story Continues
by Robert Butler

ISBN 1 84002 534 4   £1.50

OOKS

Books by Peter Hall

Shakespeare's Advice to the Players

'Acting students and young professionals will flock to learn from him... passionate, entertaining... Indisputably wise and true... Wonderfully illuminating' *Daily Telegraph*

'As fascinating to readers as it is to actors' *Independent*

| ISBN 1 84002 411 9 | £9.99 | (paperback) |
| ISBN 1 84002 372 4 | £19.99 | (hardback) |

Exposed by the Mask: Form and Language in Drama

'The wisest and most stimulating short book about theatre since Peter Brook's *The Empty Space*' Charles Spencer, *Sunday Telegraph*

| ISBN 1 84002 182 9 | £7.99 | (paperback) |
| ISBN 1 84002 142 X | £9.99 | (hardback) |

The Autobiography of Peter Hall: Making an Exhibition of Myself

'Compulsive stuff' *Independent*

ISBN 1 84002 115 2   £12.99

Peter Hall's Diaries: The Story of a Dramatic Battle
Edited by John Goodwin

'This is a stupendous book. It is the most absorbing book on the theatre I have ever read' Harold Hobson, *Sunday Times*

ISBN 1 84002 102 0   £15.99

For more information on these and other titles published by Oberon Books visit our website: www.oberonbooks.com